German-American Genealogical Research
Monograph Number 12

EMIGRANTS FROM THE FORMER AMT DAMME, OLDENBURG, (NOW NIEDERSACHSEN), GERMANY, MAINLY TO THE UNITED STATES, 1830–1849

Clifford Neal Smith

CLEARFIELD

Reprint, December 1985 √
Reprint, November 1986 √
Reprint, December 1986 ±
Reprint, January 1987 ±ʃ
Reprint, May 1988 qz
Reprint, November 1989 qz
Reprint, December 1992 qz
Reprint, November 1994 u

Originally published
McNeal, Arizona, 1981

Reprinted for
Clearfield Company, Inc. by
Genealogical Publishing Co., Inc.
Baltimore, Maryland
2004

International Standard Book Number: 0-8063-5259-0

Made in the United States of America

INTRODUCTION

Emigration from northwestern Germany began to take on noticeable proportion only after 1830. Before then, emigration had been mostly seasonal and mainly to Holland, with annual or eventual return of the migrant laborers to their home villages. As a consequence, this list of emigrants from the former Amt Damme (administrative office) of Oldenburg is probably nearly complete, as it pertains to overseas migrants.[1] The list was originally prepared by Johannes Ostendorf from official files[2] and published in an article entitled "Zur Geschichte der Auswanderung aus dem alten Amt Damme (Oldb.) insbesondere nach Nordamerika, in den Jahren 1830-1880," in *Oldenburger Jahrbuch*, vol. 46/47 (1942/1943), appearing on pages 164-279. Herr Ostendorf's article includes a good deal of historical, statistical, and sociological material not included in this monograph.

The territory of the former Amt Damme had traditionally belonged to Niederstift Muenster, a conglomeration of estates belonging to the Archbishopric of Muenster. Thus, there was a large percentage of the population which remained Roman Catholic, despite the general predominance of Lutherans in northern Germany after the Reformation. In 1803 the Niederstift, including Damme, Vechta, Cloppenburg, and Friesoythe, fell to Oldenburg. After a reorganization of administrative offices in 1814, Damme was joined with Lohne, Dinklage, Neuenkirchen, and Steinfeld villages to make the administrative district of Amt Steinfeld. In 1817, after a border change between Hannover and Oldenburg, Damme and Neuenkirchen became known as Amt Damme. Holdorf was removed from the new *Amt* in 1827. In 1871 Damme and what remained of Amt Steinfeld were again merged, but in 1879 all the area was combined with Amt Vechta.

For the purposes of this list, however, the "former Amt Damme" includes the *Gemeinden* (townships) of Damme, Holdorf, and Neuenkirchen, without considering the above-described political changes. For researchers who may be disappointed in not finding an ancestor listed herein, a search of the Vechta records might be productive.

It should be remarked that this list contains the names of a group of emigrants from Damme under the leadership of Franz Joseph Stallo who settled first in Cincinnati and more permanently in Stallotown (later Minster) in Auglaize County, Ohio. Others settled at Fort Jennings, Putnam County.

Ostendorf goes into considerable detail regarding the economic and social plight of the *Heuerleute* (hired people) in Oldenburg, who comprised most of the migrants. Population growth, changing agricultural methods, perhaps falling prices for agricultural products, caused a significant decline in the availability of jobs for these unattached people, and migration to a more promising area became the only alternative to starvation.

---

1. One exception is Johann Bernard Steinemann from Osterdamme (born 13 September 1767, the son of Johann Steinemann and Maria Anna Weinholt) who emigrated via Holland to Boston in his youth. He died in Boston before 1835, and his heirs were sought in Damme thereafter.

2. The following administrative files have been consulted: Landratsamt Vechta: Akte A.III.7 (Betr. Bevoelkerungspolizei. Auswanderungen, insbesonders die darueber aufzustellenden Listen. Generalia und Specialia. Amt Damme); A.III.7 (Betr. Auswanderungen. Amt Vechta. 2. Convolut.); A.III.8 (Betr. Austritt aus dem Staatsverband. 3. Convolut. Amt Damme); A.III.8 (Betr. Auswanderungen 1851-1870. Altes Amt Damme. 3. Convolut. Regiminalia und Specialia); A.III.9 (Betr. Austritt aus dem Staatsverband. Amt Vechta. 3 Convolut. Regiminalia und Specialia); A.III.10 (Betr. Verhandlungen mit auswaertigen Behoerden ueber Staatsangehoerigkeit. Amt Damme. Regiminalia); A.IV.d6 (Betr. Auswanderungen. Amt Damme. 4. Convolut.); DAI19 (Militaersachen. Akte betr. Einleitung des gerichtlichen Verfahrens gegen ausgewanderte Militaerpflichtige. Generalia und Specialia). Staatsarchiv Oldenburg: Bestand 70 (Regierung), XI2c (Betr. Wiedereinfuehrung der Legge-Anstalten im Amte Damme. Anstellung von Leggemeistern). Staatsarchiv Osnabrueck: Rep. 116I, Nr.4246. Congregational Archives: Church registers of Damme, Holdorf, and Neuenkirchen parishes. Zentralstelle fuer Kirchenbuchauskuenfte in Vechta: Notarized abstracts from various parish registers. [Various published works and newspapers were also used in the compilation.]

Borringhausen Farming Community

ROTTINGHAUS, Johann Bernhard, s of Johann Heinrich Rottinghaus;
    dom. Elking farm   1/1832

ROTTINGHAUS, Johann Heinrich, s of Friedrich Rottinghaus; dom.
    Elking farm   1/1833

ROTTINGHAUS, Friedrich, with d Maria Elisabeth Rottinghaus; dom.
    Elking farm   2/1839

ROTTINGHAUS, Catharina Maria, d of Johann Heinrich Rottinghaus;
    dom. Elking farm   1/1839

LAMPE, Johann Heinrich; dom. Elking farm   1/1844

IMSIEKE, Engel, b VENNEMANN, widow, with her s; dom. Sextro farm
    2/1832

DIEKHUES, Friedrich, with w Elisabeth Diekhues, b AUSTING; dom.
    Sextro farm   2/1833

PIENING, Johann Bernhard, with w -- Piening, b ROENNEKER; dom.
    Sextro farm   2/1833

FELDMANN, Johann Heinrich, with w Adelheid Feldmann, b DIEKHUES,
    & 2 dd; dom. Sextro farm   4/1834

KUHLMANN, Friedrich, with w Elisabeth Kuhlmann, b PIENING, &
    foster c Anna Maria LANGE; dom. Sextro farm   3/1835

MOORMANN, Heinrich, with w Engel Moormann, b GEISE, & 2 ss &
    2 dd; dom. Sextro farm   6/1839

BERTING, Carl; dom. Sextro farm   1/1839

LANGE, Maria; dom. Sextro farm   1/1843

MACKE, Maria; dom. Sextro farm   1/1843

GAUSEPOHL, Johann Bernard, with w Anna Maria Gausepohl, b
    FISCHER, with cc Heinrich, Franz, Agnes, & Maria Anna;
    dom. Sextro farm   6/1833

BUSCH, Hermann Heinrich; Rohling farm   1/1832

1

Borringhausen Farming Community (continued)

SCHROEDER, Johann Bernard; Rohling farm   1/1832

BUSCH, Johann Bernard, Maria Engle, & Anna Maria, siblings; dom.
    Rohling farm   3/1833

NIEHUES, Johann Heinrich; dom. Rohling farm   1/1833

IHLENDORF, Johann Heinrich; dom. Rohling farm   1/1833

GEISE, Arnold Heinrich & Maria Elisabeth, siblings; dom. Rohling
    farm   2/1833

GAUSEPOHL, Anna Maria; dom. Rohling farm   1/1833

SCHROEDER, Christopher, Maria Engel, & Bernardina, siblings;
    dom. Rohling farm   3/1833

BUSCH, Catharina Maria, widow, & her son-in-law Friedrich ROTTING-
    HAUS, with w Elisabeth Rottinghaus, b Busch, & s Johann Hein-
    rich; dom. Rohling farm   4/1834

SCHROEDER, Friedrich, miller at the windmill, with w Engel
    Schroeder, b HUENINGHAKE, & 2 ss & 2 dd; dom. Rohling
    farm   6/1834

GAUSEPOHL, Johann Heinrich, with w Elisabeth Gausepohl, b BAUNE,
    & their remaining cc Johann Bernard, Maria Agnes, Carl, &
    Elisabeth; dom. Rohling farm   6/1835

SCHROEDER, Johann Heinrich, blacksmith, with w Anna Maria
    Schroeder, b HORST, & ss Heinrich, Josef, & Friedrich;
    dom. Rohling farm   5/1839

NIEHUS, Christopher; dom. Rohling farm   1/1841

RONNEBAUM, Johann Bernard; dom. Kruthaupt farm   1/1832

PRUENE, Anna Maria & Maria Elisabeth, sisters; dom Kruthaupt
    farm   2/1833

RONNEBAUM, Johann Heinrich; dom Kruthaupt farm   1/1833

RONNEBAUM, Johann Hermann, with w Maria Engel Ronnebaum, b
    IMSIEKE, & youngest s Friedrich; dom Kruthaupt farm   3/1835

Borringhausen Farming Community (continued)

ROEMER, Johann Heinrich, with w -- Roemer, b OSTERHOFF, & d Agnes;
    dom. Kruthaupt farm   3/1839

TRENKAMP, Josef, with w Catharina Maria Trenkamp, b WIELENBERG,
    & d Agnes; dom. Kruthaupt farm   3/1844

IMSIEKE, Maria Agnes; dom. Macke farm   1/1833

TRENKAMP, Christian Heinrich, with w Maria Trenkamp, b IMSIEKE,
    & cc Heinrich & Maria Elisabeth; dom. Macke farm   4/1835

BOVING, Johann Heinrich, with w Anna Maria Boving, b IMSIEKE,
    & d Anna Maria; dom. Rasche farm   3/1835

HERMESCH, Maria Elisabeth & Catharina, siblings; dom. Rasche
    farm   2/1839

BUSCH, Johann Bernard; dom. Strieker farm   1/1833

HEIDKAMP, Heinrich, with w -- Heidkamp, b TRIMPE; dom. Strieker
    farm   2/1833

BUSCH, Franz; dom. Strieker farm   1/1841

FELDMANN, Johann Bernard, with w Agnes Feldmann, b BAUNE, &
    3 dd & 1 s; dom. Meyer farm   6/1842
AUSTING, Johann Bernard & Agnes, siblings; dom. Osterhoff farm
                                             2/1843

MICHAEL, Agnes; dom. Osterhoff farm   1/1843

SCHMIESING, Johann Bernard; dom. Middelkamp farm   1/1833

MIDDELKAMP, Johann Heinrich, s of farmowner -- Middelkamp   1/1835

BAEUMER, Johann Heirnich, widower, with s Johann Heinrich
    Baeumer, with w Anna Maria Baeumer, b ASHORN, & their
    cc Josef & Maria Anna; dom. Middelkamp farm   5/1835

SUENNEBERG, --, b SUNNERHUES, widow, with her cc Franz & Dina
    & her sister Elisabeth [Sunnerhues?]; dom. Schroeder farm 4/1832

BORGERDING, Hermann Heinrich, with w Elisabeth Borgerding, b
    BAUNE, & 2 ss & 1 d; dom. Schroeder farm   5/1842

4

Borringhausen Farming Community (continued)

MOORMANN, Josef, born in Damme; dom. Schroeder cottage   1/1843

ESCHHAKE, --, widow and cottage owner, with her cc Friedrich,
    Bernard, Agnes, & Elisabeth; dom. Eschhake cottage   5/1841

POHLSCHNEIDER, Friedrich & Maria Elisabeth, siblings; dom.
    Pohlschneider cottage   2/1832

POHLSCHNEIDER, Friedrich, widower & cottage owner, with his
    remaining cc Johann Heinrich, Jakob Josef, Maria Agnes,
    & Franz; dom. Pohlschneider cottage   5/1833

ENNEKING, Hermann Heinrich, with w Elisabeth Enneking, b
    IHLENDORF & 1 c; dom. Pohlschneider cottage   3/1836

MESSMANN, Heinrich, with w Elisabeth Messmann, b SCHROEDER,
    & 1 c; dom. Pohlschneider cottage   3/1836

MEYER, Werner; dom. Pohlschneider cottage   1/1836

DECKER, Heinrich, with w Engel Decker, b MESSMANN; dom. Pohl-
    schneider cottage   2/1839

WELLMANN, Johann Bernard & Elisabeth, siblings; dom. Pohl-
    schneider cottage   2/1844

PILLE, Johann Bernard & Johann Heinrich, brothers; dom. Lien-
    land cottage   2/1833

PILLE, Elisabeth, Anna Maria, & Friedrich, siblings; Lienland
    cottage   3/1843

HOGREFE, Franz, with w Agnes Hogrefe, b VENNEMANN, d Maria Anna
    & foster child Anna Maria Engel IMSIEKE; dom. Hoelterhin-
    richs cottage   4/1835

BROKAMP, Catharina Maria, with 1 c of her brother Johann Hein-
    rich Brokamp; dom. Hoelterhinrichs cottage   2/1835

SCHMIDT, --, widow, with 1 s; dom. Hoelterhinrichs cottage   2/1835

BROKAMP, Anna Maria & Hermann [siblings?]; dom. Hoelterhinrichs
    cottage   2/1838

SCHMIESING, Anna Maria; dom. Hoelterhinrichs cottage   1/1838

Borringhausen Farming Community (continued)

SCHILDMEYER, Agnes; dom. Hoelterhinrichs   1/1839

HELMKAMP, Christopher, with w Anna Maria Helmkamp, b MEYROSE, &
    4 dd & 2 ss; dom. Hoelterhinrichs cottage   8/1841

KLOSTERMANN, --, with w Anna Maria Klostermann, b WIELENBERG,
    & 1 c; dom. Lindemann cottage   3/1841

FRANKE, Christian, with w Anna Maria Franke, b BUSCH, & 1 c;
    dom. Wiehebrink cottage   3/1838

SUNNERHUES, Anna Maria, with d Elisabeth; dom. Luermann cottage
                                                                       2/1842

WIELENBERG, Maria Agnes; dom. Wielenberg cottage   1/1832

HERMESCH, Maria Agnes; dom. Hermesch cottage   1/1833

HUELSMANN, Maria Elisabeth; dom. Huelsmann cottage   1/1839

HUELSMANN, Christopher & Bernard [brothers?]; dom. Huelsmann
    cottage   2/1843

LUETMERDING, Johann Bernard; dom. Huelsmann cottage   1/1843

BAEUMER, Johann Bernard, cottage owner, with w Maria Elisabeth
    Baeumer, b SUNNERHUES, & ss Heinrich & Bernard; dom.
    Baeumer cottage   4/1833

HEIDLAGE, Johann Bernard, wagonmaker, with w Elisabeth Heidlage,
    b STALLO; dom. Baeumer cottage   2/1844

HELLEBUSCH, Franz; dom. Baeumer cottage   1/1844

IHLENDORF, Johann Heinrich, with w Anna Mara Ihlendorf, b ESCH-
    HAKE, & cc Johann Heinrich, Johann Heinrich[!] & Friedrich;
    dom. Baeumer cottage   5/1835

BORGERDING, Franz, with w Anna Maria Borgerding, b BAUNE; dom.
    Meschlueke cottage   2/1845

BROKAMP, Josef [& one other?]   2/1845

SCHILDMEYER, Maria   1/1845

Borringhausen Farming Community (continued)

SCHWENKER, N. N., from brother-in-law's guardianship? [aus *Schwa-gers Leibzucht*] 1/1845

AUSTING, Bernard, & sister 2/1845

LANGE, Heinrich 1/1846

HELLEBUSCH, — [and 1 other] 2/1846

WIETHORN, Josef 1/1846

BORGERDING, Heinrich 1/1846

SCHMIESING, Elisabeth, & her sister 2/1846

MACKE, Bernard, hand laborer; destination Baltimore 1/1847

HEITLAGE, Ferdinand, hand laborer; destination Baltimore 1/1847

HEITLAGE, Agnes, maid; destination Baltimore 1/1847

MACKE, Heinrich, hired hand; destination Cincinnati 1/1848

BLOEMER [*or* BOEHNER], Bernard, farmowner, with w & 4 cc; destination Cincinnati 6/1848

ENNEKING, Maria, maid; destination Cincinnati 1/1848

BAEUMER, Elisabeth, widow, with 3 cc under 14 years of age; destination Baltimore 4/1849

LAMPE, Bernard, hired hand; destination Baltimore 1/1849

MACKE, Elisabeth, maid; destination Baltimore 1/1849

GAUSEPOHL, Elisabeth, maid; destination Baltimore 1/1849

MICHAEL, Christian, hand laborer; destination Baltimore 1/1849

HOGREFE, Agnes, maid; destination Baltimore 1/1849

Damme Village

STALLO, Franz, with 5 cc	6/1830
NORDHOFF, Maria Anna	1/1834
CORDEMEYER, Franz	1/1836
NORDHOFF, Martin	1/1842
BUSCH, Agnes	1/1840
BUSCH, Maria Anna	1/1840
FISCHER, Friedrich	1/1836
SCHNITKER, Heinrich	1/1834
PIEPER, Christopher	1/1832
PIEPER, Bernard, property owner, with 1 c	2/1842
BAEUMER, --, widow, with 5 cc	6/1838
GARRE, Bernard	1/1842
IN DER RIEDEN, Anton, property owner, with w & 2 cc	4/1838
GRIMME, Franz	1/1832
EBERLE, Heinrich	1/1836
EBERLE, Lisette & Jenne, with 1 c	3/1842
TEPE, Heinrich & Elisabeth	2/1840
TEPE, Berend	1/1836
WESSEL, Clemens	1/1836
MAEHLER, Hermann, with 3 cc	4/1836
SCHILDMEYER, Anna Maria	1/1842
MOORMANN, Josef	1/1842
MERKEL, August	1/1838

Damme Village (continued)

PIEPER, Julie	1/1842
CASSO, Franz	1/1842
WICHELMANN, Heinrich	1/1844
STRICKER, Johann Heinrich, property owner, with w & 5 cc	7/1835
VON DER HEYDE, Franz, Anton, Josef, & Carl	4/1836
RASCHE, Heinrich & Rudolf	2/1841
POETKER, --, with w & 3 cc	5/1834
MACKE, Wilhelm	1/1844
HARIG, --, 2 ss & 2 dd of	4/1836
MUEGGENBORG, Anna Maria	1/1844
DEYER, Johann Heinrich, with 3 dd	4/1844
KROGMANN, Johann Heinrich, with w & 1 c	3/1844
WIENER, Heinrich, property owner, with w & 4 cc	6/1844
FISCHER, Berend, with w & 5 cc	7/1836
DECKER, --, widow, with 2 dd & 3 ss	6/1835
ROSEMEYER, --, blacksmith, with w & 6 cc	8/1835
ROSEMEYER, Fritz & Anton	2/1836
BOERGER, Hinderich, with w & 5 cc	7/1834
VON DER HEIDE, Hermann	1/1836
FISCHER, Heinrich, with w & 6 cc	8/1836
DECKER, Franz, 2 ss of	2/1836
BROKAMP, Elisabeth	1/1844
TECKER, --, widow, 2 ss & 1 d of	3/1838

Damme Village (continued)

SCHUMACHER, Eilert & Elisabeth	2/1832
STRIEKER, Maria Anna	1/1844
STEINEMANN, Maria	1/1834
BOERGER, Caspar, s & d of	2/1830
BOLKE, --, with w & 2 cc	4/1832
NORDHOFF, Elisabeth	1/1844
SCHIWSCHEWSKI, Carolina	1/1844
NORDHOFF, Agnes	1/1842
ESCHHAKE, Agnes	1/1840
NIEHAUS, Christopher	1/1840
IMSIEKE, Josef	1/1836
KROEGER, Berend	1/1836
BOERGER, Heinrich Christopher	1/1838
BOERGER, Josef	1/1838
ENNEKING, Josef	1/1839
ROTTINGHAUS, Heinrich	1/1843
FLOTTEMESCH, Josef	1/1840
BARHORST, Margaretha	1/1830
KOHS, Agnes, *Greten* [meaning unknown]	1/1840
GRUETNER, Heinrich	1/1836
MEYER, Werner	1/1840
GEHES, Berend	1/1840
FREKING, Berend Friedrich, Agnes, & Dina	3/1836

Damme Village (continued)

BUSCH, --, watchmaker, with w & 1 c	3/1834
HUESMANN, Friedrich	1/1843
SCHARWALL, Theresia	1/1835
FREKE, Franz	1/1835
ABEL, Josef	1/1834
IN DER RIEDEN, --, with 3 cc	4/1833
HUESMANN, Wilhelm	1/1834
MORHUES, --, with w & 1 c	3/1837
WILKE, --, widow, with 4 cc	5/1842
ROSEMEYER, Dina & Josefina	2/1844
PUTTHOFF, Hermann	1/1830
BOLKE, Agnes	1/1844
MEYROSE, Berend	1/1844
SCHUETTE, Berend, with w & 2 cc	4/1838
IN DER RIEDEN, Franz & Clemens	2/1840
HAVERBECK, Anton	1/1832
NIEHAUS, Hinrich	1/1842
NORDHOFF, Anton	1/1832
SCHILDMEYER, Gertrud	1/1844
DETMER, --, with w & 2 cc	4/1834
IHLENDORF, Elisabeth	1/1834
GAUSEPOHL, --, with w & 4 cc	6/1832

Damme Village (continued)

DEYE, Johann Heinrich	1/1845
BROKAMP, Berend	1/1845
BROKAMP, Anna Maria	1/1845
VISCHNEWSKI, Caroline	1/1845
NORDHOFF, Elisabeth	1/1845
DECKER, Franz, with w & d	3/1845
WIENER, Anton, with w & d	3/1845
DECKER, Heinrich, with w & s	3/1845
BOERGER, Berend	1/1845
BOERGER, Elisabeth	1/1845
KRAMER, Heinrich, with w & d	3/1845
DEYE, Anna Maria	1/1845
DEYE, Theresia	1/1845
DEYE, Gottfried	1/1845
STRIEKER, --, girl with illegitimate c	2/1846
SCHILDMEYER, --, total of	3/1846
BROKAMP, --, hired hand, total of	5/1846
SCHUMACHER, Carolina, farmowner, took 50 Reichsthaler with her; destination Baltimore	1/1847
STRIEKER, Franz, hand laborer; destination Baltimore	1/1847
STRIEKER, Heinrich & Bernard, hired hands; destination Baltimore	2/1847
ROBKE, Bernd, farmowner and landowner; took 40 Reichsthaler with him; destination Baltimore	1/1847

Damme Village (continued)

BOERGER, Maria, maid; destination Baltimore   1/1847

BOERGER, Anton, hand laborer; destination Baltimore   1/1847

BUSCH, Berend, hand laborer & landowner, with s; destination
    Baltimore   2/1847

BOECKER, Dina, without profession; took 100 Reichsthaler with her;
    destination Baltimore   1/1847

MOORMANN, Fritz & Josef, hand laborer, landowner; took 100 Reichs-
    thaler with them; destination Baltimore   2/1847

ROSEMEYER, Josefine, farmowner; destination Cincinnati   1/1847

FUESTING, Josef, hired hand; destination Cincinnati   1/1847

KLAUSING, Fritz "little," hand laborer; destination Cincinnati
                                                             1/1847

ROENKER, Lisette, maid; destination Cincinnati   1/1847

TEPE, Heinrich, hired hand; destination Baltimore   1/1848

TEPE, Werner, hired hand; destination Baltimore   1/1848

ROENKER, Bernard, hired hand; destination Baltimore   1/1848

ROENKER, Lisette, maid; destination Baltimore   1/1848

DRAHMANN, Maria, maid; destination Baltimore   1/1848

WITTKORN, Bernd, "little," hired hand; destination Baltimore 1/1848

MEYER, Maria Anna, maid; destination Baltimore   1/1848

SEXTRO, Christopher, farmowner and landowner; destination
    Cincinnati   1/1848

STALL, Georg, no profession; destination Cincinnati   1/1848

NORDHOFF, Bernd, farmer & landowner; with w & 1 c under 15
    years; destination Cincinnati   3/1848

Damme Village (continued)

EILERMANN, Franz, hand laborer; destination Cincinnati 1/1848

KRAMER, Fritz, hired hand; took 200 Reichsthaler with him;
 destination Cincinnati 1/1848

PIEPER, Lisette, maid; destination Cincinnati 1/1848

WIELENBERG, Heinrich, hand laborer; destination Cincinnati 1/1848

BACK, Josef, hand laborer; destination Cincinnati 1/1848

FREDE, Clemens, hand laborer; destination Cincinnati 1/1848

ROSEMEYER, Clemens, peasant; destination Cincinnati 1/1848

BAEUMER, Bernard, hand laborer; destination Cincinnati 1/1848

SACK, Maria, no profession; destination Baltimore 1/1848

BOERGER, Heinrich, farmer, with [w?] & 1 c over 15 years;
 destination Cincinnati 3/1849

WITTKORN, Bernard "little," no profession; destination Cincinnati 1/1849

FUESTING, Agnes, maid; destination Cincinnati 1/1849

CANISIUS, --, woman & c under 15 years, peasants; took 300
 Reichsthaler with them; destination Cincinnati 2/1849

Duemmerlohausen Farming Community

MOORMANN, Bernd, hired hand, with 5 cc; dom. Meyer farm 6/1833

FLOCKMANN, Bernd, hired hand, with w & 2 cc; dom. Meyer farm 4/1833

SCHMIESING, Bernd, hired hand, with w & 2 cc; dom. Meyer farm
 4/1841

GREFENKAMP, Bernd, hired hand, the 4 cc of; dom. Meyer farm 4/1841

Duemmerlohausen Farming Community (continued)

WIETHORN, Hermann, hired hand, with w & 2 cc; dom. Meyer farm
4/1841

LANGE, --, farmer, 3 cc of   3/1843

DECKER, Nikolaus, hired hand, d of; dom. Robke cottage   1/1834

WIETHORN, Hermann, hired hand, s of; dom. Wempe cottage   1/--

WIEHEBRING, --, cottage owner, with w & 4 cc   6/1833

LANGE, Christian, hired hand, 3 cc of; Moormann farm   3/1842

WESSEL, Johann Heinrich, hired hand, 2 cc of; Moormann farm   2/1842

HUENINGHAKE, Engel; dom. Moormann farm   1/1842

BOLLER, Johann Heinrich, cottage owner, 2 cc of   2/1840

HONKOMP [so spelled] --, widow, with 3 cc; dom. Boller cottage   4/1843

MEYROSE, Gerhard, hired hand, with 2 cc; dom. Boller cottage 3/1843

FISCHER, --, farm owner, with w & 1 c   3/1836

BAEUMER, --, cottage owner, 1 c of   1/1836

WOLKING, --, cottage owner, 1 c of   1/1833

GREVER, Friedrich, hired hand, with w & 1 c; dom. Wolking cottage   3/1833

GEISE, --, cottage owner, 2 cc of   2/1833

HUENINGHAKE, --, hired hand & widow, with 3 cc; dom. Jost-
Enneking farm   4/1833

HUMPER, --, hired hand, with w; Jost-Enneking farm   2/1833

WIENHOLD, Bernd, hired hand, with w & 2 cc; dom. Jost-Enneking
farm   4/1839

STEINRIEDE, Bernd, hired hand, 6 cc of; Jost-Enneking farm   6/1841

Duemmerlohausen Farming Community (continued)

BROKAMP, --, cottager, 3 cc of   3/1840

ARLING, --, cottager, 3 cc of   3/1838

WIENHOLD, Heinrich, hired hand, with w & 3 cc; dom. Arling
    cottage   5/1837

STRIEKER, --, with bride; dom. Arling cottage   2/1840

HUENINGHAKE, Bernd, hired hand, with w & 2 cc; dom. Arling
    cottage   4/1842

VON DER HEIDE, --, hired hand, s of; dom. Auf der Tangen
    farm   1/1832

MEYER, --, hired hand, s of; dom. Auf der Tangen farm   1/1838

STEINEMANN, Hermann Heinrich, hired hand, with w & 2 cc;
    dom. Tangemann cottage   4/1837

STEINEMANN, Heinrich, hired hand, with w & 2 cc; dom.
    Tangemann cottage   4/1832

STEINEMANN, --, cottager, brother of   1/1836

FISCHER, Engel, d of hired hand; dom. Kessing cottage   1/1839

MACKE, Heinrich, s of hired hand; dom. Kessing cottage   1/1843

DALINGHUS, Bernd, hired hand, with w & 3 cc; dom. Wolking
    farm   5/1842

BAEUMER, --, widow, s of; dom. Wolking farm   1/1842

MACKE, --, hired hand, 2 ss of; dom. Wolking farm   2/1842

BROKAMP, --, hired hand, s of; dom. Wolking farm   1/1833

VON DER HEIDE, Hermann, hired hand, with w & 5 cc; dom.
    Wolking farm   7/1836

BEI DER HAKE, Bernd, hired hand, with w & 1 c; dom. Robke
    farm   3/1841

Duemmerlohausen Farming Community (continued)

GEERS, --, widow, hired hand, with 4 cc; dom. Robke farm   5/1841

DIEKHAUS, --, widow, hired hand, with 2 cc; dom. ?   3/1833

ENNEKING, --, hired hand, with w & 2 cc; dom. Robke farm   4/1833

ENNEKING, --, 2 brothers of farm owner -- Enneking   2/1831

ENNEKING, Bernd, hired hand, with w & 5 cc; dom. Enneking
    farm   7/1835

FISCHER, Heinrich, hired hand, with w & 1 c; dom. Enneking
    farm   3/1841

MEYER, --, window, hired hand, with 3 cc; dom. Ennking farm   4/1839

TANGEMANN, --, hired hand, with w & 3 cc; dom. Ennking farm   5/1834

KLAENE, --, hired hand, with w & 3 cc; dom. Enneking farm   5/1835

ENNEKING, --, d of Werneken Enneking, hired hand; dom. Enne-
    king farm   1/1838

TRIMPE, Hermann Heinrich, s of -- Trimpe, hired hand; dom.
    Enneking farm   1/1834

WIETHORN, Hermann, with bride; dom. Enneking farm   2/1842

RONNEBAUM, --, 2 cc of farmowner -- Ronnebaum   2/1840

MOORMANN, --, 2 cc of -- Moormann, widow; dom. Suing in Ol-
    dorf   2/1839

MACKE, --, d of -- Macke, hired hand; dom. Lamping farm   1/1838

BECKMANN, --, hired hand, with w & 2 cc; dom. Lamping farm   4/1834

AUSTING, --, 2 sisters; dom. Lamping farm   2/1839

TANGEMANN, --, hired hand, with w & 2 cc; dom. Lamping farm   4/1837

WIEHEBRING, Berend Heinrich, & his sister; dom. ?   2/1845

LAMPING, Bernard, s of Heinrich Lamping; dom. ?   1/1845

Duemmerlohausen Farming Community (continued)

GEERS, --, d of -- Geers in Oldorf   1/1845

TEPE, --, widow; dom. ?   1/1845

MESCHER, Hermann, with w & 1 c; dom. ?   3/1845

PARDIEK, --, with w & 1 c; dom. ?   3/1845

WIEHEBRING, Hermann Heinrich, with w & 1 c; dom. ?   3/1845

ENNEKING, --, [woman]   1/1845

LANGE, Christian, hired hand; destination Baltimore   1/1847

MACKE, --, widow, with 2 ss & 1 d; destination Baltimore   4/1848

WIETHARN, Franz, farmer, with w; took 50 Reichsthaler with
    them; destination Cincinnati   2/1848

FLOCKMANN, Elisabeth, maid; destination Cincinnati   1/1848

MEYER, Theresia, maid; destination Cincinnati   1/1848

LANGE, Franz, with 4 cc over 15 years old; destination Balti-
    more   5/1848

TRENKAMP, Heinrich, hand worker, with w; took 50 Reichsthaler
    with them; destination Baltimore   2/1848

PARDIEK, --, family with 1 s over 15 years; took 150 Reichs-
    thaler with them; destination Baltimore   3/1848

KRAMER, Maria, maid; took 100 Reichsthaler with her; destina-
    tion Baltimore   1/1848

Holte Farming Community

NIENHAUS, Heinrich, with family; dom. by Meyer Holzgrefe in
    Bokern   4/1844

MEYER, Elisabeth; dom. by Meyer Holzgrefe in Bokern   1/1837

18

Holte Farming Community (continued)

GREFENKAMP, --, widow of Heinrich Grefenkamp, with family; dom.
   Meyer in Holte   5/1838

GREFENKAMP, Bernd Heinrich, with family; dom. Meyer in Holte 4/1838

SEEP, --, d of Bernard Seep; dom. Niehaus farm   1/1842

DALINGHAUS, --, widow of Wilke Dalinghaus, with d   2/1842

ARKENBERG, Heinrich, hired hand; destination Cincinnati   1/1848

ARKENBERG, Elisabeth, maid; destination Cincinnati   1/1848

Osterdamme Farming Community

ASSMANN, Bernd; dom. with Brinkhoff   1/1834

FELDKAMP, Heinrich, with w; dom. Klausing farm   2/1836

ADELMEYER, Bernard Heinrich, with w & 4 cc; dom. with Salker 6/1836

BROKAMP, Franz, with w & 1 c; dom. with Fischer   3/1837

ROBKE, Maria; dom. with Boving   1/1844

SIEVERDING, Caspar, brother of farmowner -- Sieverding   1/1834

STEINEMANN, Bernard, brother of cottage owner -- Steinemann 1/1836

ASSMANN, Bernard, brother of cottage owner -- Assmann   1/1834

MEESMANN, Heinrich, with w, 2 brothers-in-law, & mother-in-
   law; dom. with Schaeper   5/1838

ROTTINGHAUS, Wilhelm, house owner, with w & 5 cc   7/1834

BRINKHOFF, Maria; dom. with Thoele   1/1844

MACKE, Herm[ann], with w & 1 c; dom. with "little' Berting 3/1844

LIENLAND, Bernard, house owner   1/1834

Osterdamme Farming Community (continued)

MEYER, --, widow, with 3 cc; dom. Macke farm   4/1833

LIENLAND, Fritz, house owner?   1/1832

THIELE, Gerhard, with w & 4 cc; dom. Macke farm   6/1835

ROLFES, Fritz; dom. with Macke   1/1838

LUENING, --, master tailor; dom. with Mackeliening   1/1842

KROEGER, Dina; dom. with Mackeliening   1/1844

ASSMANN, Heinrich, with w, 3 cc, mother-in-law, & brother-in-
        law; dom. with Mackeliening   7/1834

FISCHER, Heinrich, with w & 5 cc; dom. with Berting   7/1834

WOEHRMANN, Heinrich, with w & 1 c; dom. with Wellerding   3/1836

KRUSE, --, widow; dom. with Wellerding   1/1843

FELDMANN, Agnes; dom. with Wellerding   1/1837

STRIEKER, Agnes & Elisabeth; dom. with Wellerding   2/1839

KRUSE, Engel; dom. with Wellerding   1/1836

ASSMANN, Heinrich, with w & 3 cc; dom. with Frerking   5/1835

WIENHOLD, Maria; dom. with Frerking   1/1838

WIENHOLD, Engel; dom. with Frerking   1/1842

WIENHOLD, Fritz; dom. with Frerking   1/1844

ROTTINGHAUS, Agnes; dom. with Frerking   1/1843

KUHLMANN, Bernard, house owner? in Suedfelde [south fields]   1/1832

BERTING, Heinrich; dom. with Berting   1/1835

MEESMANN, Caspar, with w & 1 c; dom. Schaeper farm   3/1845

MOENKER, Bernd & Heinrich; dom. Ricking farm   2/1845

Osterdamme Farming Community (continued)

TECKER, Elisabeth; dom. Ricking farm   1/1845

STEINEMANN, Marianne, sister of cottage owner -- Steinemann   1/1845

MOEHRING, Lisette; dom. Macke farm   1/1845

MEYROSE, Heinrich; dom. Wellerding farm   1/1845

STALLO, Bernd; dom. Kamping (Kampe) farm   1/1845

DIEKHAUS, --, s & d of hired hand -- Diekhaus   2/1846

ROBKE, --, d of Gerhard Robke   1/1846

MENKE, --, maid, from Greven   1/1846

RONNEBAUM, Heinrich & Mariana, hired hand & maid respectively;
    destination Baltimore   2/1847

DIEKHAUS, Friedrich, hired hand; destination Baltimore   1/1847

Osterfeine Farming Community

Putthoff, Henrich; dom. Meyer farm   1/1840

LEHMKUHLE, Bernd, with w; dom. Meyer farm   2/1839

LUETMERDING, Henrich, with w; dom. Arkenberg farm   2/1834

JANZEN, --, widow; dom. Arkenberg farm   1/1837

HUENINGHAKE, Elisabeth; dom. Arkenberg farm   1/1844

KROEGER, Elisabeth; dom. Arkenberg farm   1/1844

DALINGHAUS, Henrich, with w & 2 cc; dom. Reinerding farm   4/1843

VON DER HEIDE, Caroline; dom. Reinerding farm   1/1843

RONNEBAUM, Ferdinand, Maria, & Elisabeth, orphans; dom. Borger-
    ding farm   3/1839

Osterfeine Farming Community (continued)

ROTTINGHAUS, Henrich; dom. Borgerding farm   1/1843

SCHULZE, Johann, Senior, with w & 2 cc, & Johann Schulze, Junior,
    with w & 3 cc; dom. "Big" Hillmann farm   9/1836

WOLTING, Henrich, s of farmowner -- Wolting   1/1838

VON HANDORF, Johann Bernard, s of houseowner -- v. Handorf   1/1837

WIETHORN, Elisabeth, orphan from Handorf   1/1843

MEYERROSE, --, widow, with 4 cc; dom. Otting cottage   5/1843

HILLMANN, Franz; dom. "little" Hillmann cottage   1/1832

BROKAMP, Franz & Hermann Henrich; dom. "little" Hillmann cot-
    tage   2/1837

LUETMERDING, Maria; dom. "little" Austing cottage   1/1843

PUTTHOFF, Heinrich, tailor, with w & 6 cc; dom. Buning farm   8/1839

LUETMERDING, --, widow, with 2 cc; dom. Buning farm   3/1844

PUTTHOFF, Bernd, tailor, with w & 2 cc; dom. Buning farm   4/1844

KRAMER, Hermann Heinrich, with w & 3 cc; dom. Buning farm   5/1844

HEITMANN, Ferdinand, Franz, ss of widow -- Heitmann   2/1839

HEITMANN, Bernd & Heinrich, ss of widow -- Heitmann   2/1844

RONNEBAUM ("Little"), Heinrich, property owner, s of -- Ronne-
    baum ("Little")   1/1832

SCHAEPER, Johann Bernd, with w & 2 cc; dom. "Little Ronnebaum
                                                                   4/1834

RONNEBAUM, Bernd, with w; dom. "Little" Ronnebaum   2/1836

MACKE, Franz, with w & d; dom. "Big" Ronnebaum   3/1831

SCHMIESING, Engel, orphan; dom. "Big" Ronnebaum   1/1844

Osterfeine Farming Community (continued)

SCHAEPER, Franz, Berndhenrich, & Ferdinand, ss of cottage owner
-- Schaeper   3/1831

BOLKE, --, widow, with d & s; dom. with Gravemeyer   3/1836

KRAMER, Clemens & Ferdinand, ss of -- Kramer   2/1836

PUTTHOFF, --, widow, with 3 cc; dom. with Kramer   4/1839

SCHROEDER, Friedrich, with w & 3 cc; dom. with Kramer   5/1839

SCHMIESING, Agnes, d of -- Schmiesing; dom. Burdiek farm   1/1844

NIEHAUS, Elisabeth & Maria; dom. Burdiek farm   2/1844

MACKE, Agnes; dom. Burdiek farm   1/1844

KUHLMANN, Bernd, s of cottage owner -- Kuhlmann   1/1832

HUENINGHAKE, Friedrich, with w; dom. Throring cottage   2/1836

THRORING, Arnold, s of cottage owner -- Throring   1/1844

AUSTING ("Little"), Bernd, with w & 2 cc; dom. Hueninghake
house   4/1836

AUSTING, Elisabeth & Heinrich, siblings; dom. Hueninghake
house   2/1838

RUSCHE, Franz, cottage owner?, with w & 6 cc   8/1834

BAEUMER, --, widow, with 1 c; dom. Haverkamp farm   2/1835

HUENINGHAKE, --, widow; dom. Haverkamp farm   1/1836

KRUSE, Henrich, with w & 2 cc; dom. Drahmann farm   4/1837

BUENNEMEYER, Franz; dom. Reinerding farm   1/1834

MACKE, Elisabeth; dom. "Little" Borgerding farm   1/1833

BURDIEK, Berndhenrich & Franz; dom. with Grefenkamp   2/1838

SCHROEDER, Caroline, Bernardine, & Henrich, siblings   3/1835

Osterfeine Farming Community (continued)

SCHROEDER, Franz, brother [of the 3 listed immediately above]
                                                        1/1844

FISCHER, Bernd; dom. Kroeger cottage   1/1844

HOLTHUS, Bernd, with w & 4 cc   6/1845

MEYER, Franz, brother of farmowner -- Meyer   .1/1845

ARKENBERG, --, s & d of farmowner -- Arkenberg   2/1845

BURDIEK, Elisabeth, d of hired hand Henrich Burdiek   1/1845

HUENINGHAKE, Elisabeth, d of house owner -- Hueninghake 1/1845

RUSCHE, Catharina Mar, d of widow -- Rusche   1/1845

WINTERMANN, Johann Henrich, s of hired hand Henrich Winter-
     mann   1/1845

LANGE, Elisabeth, d of hired hand -- Lange   1/1845

RUSCHE, Bernd, s of cottage owner -- Rusche   1/1845

SCHROEDER, Henrich, s of Bernd Schroeder of Borringhausen
     [the father had left several years before]   1/1845

SCHROEDER, Franz, s of hired hand Bernd Schroeder; dom.
     Haverkamp [farm?]   1/1846

WINTERMANN, Henrich, s of hired hand -- Wintermann; dom.
     with "Little" Putthoff   1/1846

OTTING, Elisabeth, d of hired hand & widow -- Otting; dom.
     with Meyer   1/1846

STAGGENBORG, Agnes, d of hired hand Hermann Heinrich Staggen-
     borg; dom. Suding farm   1/1846

DRAHMANN, Elisabeth, d of hired hand & widow -- Drahmann; dom.
     with Friemerding   1/1846

MACKE, Henrich, s of widow -- Macke, hired hand with Burdiek 1/1846

Osterfeine Farming Community (continued)

DETERS, Heinrich Arnold, hired hand; destination Cincinnati   1/1847

SUENNEBERG, Maria Elisabeth, maid, land owner; destination
    Cincinnati   1/1847

OSSENBECK, Bernard, hired hand; destination Baltimore   1/1847

LAMPING, Anna Maria, maid; destination Baltimore   1/1847

DROESCHER, --, married woman with s & d; destination Cincin-
    nati   3/1847

NIENABER, Elisabether, maid; destination Cincinnati   1/1847

SANDERMANN, Heinrich, farmer and hand worker; destination Cin-
    cinnati   1/1847

DRAHMANN, --, widow, with 4 cc (2 cc under 15 years); took 50
    Reichsthaler with her; destination Cincinnati   5/1848

STAGGENBORG, Caroline, hand worker & maid; destination Cincin-
    nati   1/1848

BROKAMP, Bernd, farmer, with w & 3 cc (1 under 15 years); des-
    tination Cincinnati   5/1848

MACKE, --, widow, with 3 cc (2 cc under 15 years); destination
    Cincinnati   4/1848

AUSTING "Little", Maria Annia, maid; destination Cincinnati   1/1848

KLOENNE, Engel, maid; destination Cincinnati   1/1848

WINTERMANN, Johann Heinrich, hired hand; destination Cincin-
    nati   1/1848

VON DER HEIDE, Bernd, with 6 cc (2 under 15 years); took 100
    Reichsthaler with him; destination Cincinnati   7/1848

BRINKHOFF, Maria, maid; destination Cincinnati   1/1848

RUSCHE, Bernd, hired hand; took 40 Reichsthaler with him; des-
    tination Cincinnati (to avoid military service)   1/1849

Osterfeine Farming Community (continued)

STUNTEBECK, Heinrich, hired hand; took 35 Reichsthaler with him;
     destination Cincinnati (to avoid military service)   1/1849

NIENABER, Anton, hired hand; took 45 Reichsthaler with him; des-
     tination Cincinnati (to avoid military service)   1/1849

BARLAGE, Joseph, hired hand; took 34 Reichsthaler with him; des-
     tination Cincinnati (to avoid military service)   1/1849

DETERS, Bernd, with family, 5 cc (3 cc under 15 years); destina-
     tion Cincinnati   6/1849

RABE, --, widow, with s & d (both over 15 years); destination
     Cincinnati   3/1849

STAGGENBORG, Heinrich, double family [!] each with 1 c under
     15 years & 1 c over 15 years; peasants   6/1849

DETERS, Gerhard Heinrich; dom. Haverbeck farm   1/1833

SCHRATZ, Maria Engel; dom. Trumme farm   1/1844

TRIMPE, Hermann Henrich, with w & c; dom. Trumme farm   3/1832

BERGMANN, Arnold, with w & 4 cc; dom. Trumme farm   6/1837

BERGMANN, Franz Heinrich, with w & 3 cc; dom. Trumme farm   5/1831

HOEGEMANN, Johann Heinrich, with w & 2 cc; dom. Fangmann cot-
     tage   4/1833

LOTH, --, widow, with 3 cc & mother-in-law; dom. Fangmann cot-
     tage   5/1833

MEYER, Franz Heinrich; dom. Grefenkamp cottage   1/1833

BURDIEK, Bernd Henrich; dom. Grefenkamp cottage   1/1837

DETERS, Franz Heinrich; dom. Grefenkamp cottage   1/1838

DETERS, Henrich Arnd, with w & 4 cc; dom. Grefenkamp cottage 6/1844

RABE, Maria Agnes; dom. Wielenberg cottage   1/1844

Osterfeine Farming Community (continued)

KRAMER, Maria Elisabeth; dom. Kramer house   1/1844

BECKER, Christopher, with w & 2 cc; dom. Bolke farm   4/1844

RABE, Maria; dom. Bolke farm   1/1838

MEYER, Johann Heinrich; dom. Bolke farm   1/1837

BOLKE, Hermann, widower, with 2 cc; dom. Bolke farm   3/1837

BOECKERSTETTE, Caspar, with w & 3 cc; dom. Deters farm   5/1833

MACKE, Heinrich & Maria Catharina; dom. Deters farm   2/1833

MACKE, Franz & Bernard, emigrated from Holland [by implication
     related to Heinrich & Maria Catharina Macke]   2/1837

HASKAMP, Johann Heinrich, with w & 1 c; dom. Heidkamp cottage
                                                          3/1833

SUENNEBERG, Maria Catharina; d of -- Suenneberg   1/1838

HAUSFELD, Clemens, with w, 3 cc, & father-in-law; dom. Bolke
     farm   6/1833

MACKE, Johann Bernd; dom. Bolke farm   1/1833

MEYER, Maria Engel; dom. Bolke farm   1/1833

MACKE, Clemens, brother of cottager -- Macke, emigrated from
     Holland   1/1832

BOECKERSTETTE, Heinrich, hired hand, with w & 6 cc   8/1845

Osterfeiner Half-farm: Bergfeine

SUENNEBERG, --, widow, with 4 cc; dom. Meyer farm   5/1832

FRIEMERDING, Franz, with w & 2 cc; dom. Friemerding farm   4/1832

RUSCHE, Franz, with w & 2 cc; dom. Suding farm   4/1833

Osterfeiner Half-farm: Bergfeine (continued)

SCHULTE, --, widow, with d; dom. Suding farm	2/1833
NIEHAUS, Bernard Heinrich, with w & 2 cc; dom. Putthoff farm	4/1834
GREFENKAMP, Hermann; dom. Putthoff farm	1/1833
LANGE, Bernd, with w & 7 cc; dom. Wernke farm	9/1836
KRUEMPELBECK, --, widow, with 3 cc; dom. Suding farm	4/1836
SCHMIESING, Heinrich, with w & 3 cc; dom. Suding farm	5/1844
ROHLFZEN, Bernd, with w & 3 cc; dom. Suding farm	5/1844
DROESCHER, Heinrich; dom. Gottbehoede farm	1/1844
BORGERDING, Bernd Heinrich; dom. Wernke farm	1/1844
SANDERMANN "Little", Gertrud; dom. Putthoff farm	1/1844
BRUNE, Bernd	1/1845

Reselage Farming Community

BRUNE, --, s & d of Caspar Brune; dom. Woebkenberg [cottage?]	1/1837
SCHMID, --, d of Hermann Schmid; dom. Woebkenberg [cottage?]	1/1837
WOEBKENBERG, --, s of Bernard Woebkenberg	1/1831
KUHLMANN, --, s of Heinrich Kuhlmann	1/1831
LUENING, --, cottage owner, family of	8/1843
ENNEKING, Bernard, with family; dom. Reselage farm	8/1835
IMSIEKE, Josef; dom. Reselage farm	1/1834
AUSTING, Bernard, with family; dom. Bertelt farm	5/1833
WITTKORN, Bernard, so of farmer -- Wittkorn	1/1843

28

KRAEMER, Bernard Heinrich, with family; dom. Wittkorn farm   4/1832

HERMEYER, --, widow, with 3 cc; dom. Strieker farm   4/1831

ENNEKING, --, d of Heinrich Enneking; dom. Strieker farm   1/1843

ENNEKING, Anna Maria; dom. Strieker farm   1/1843

KRUSE, --, widow, with 2 dd; dom. Lagemann farm   3/1837

RESELAGE, --, 2 dd of Friedrich Reselage; dom. Lagemann farm 2/1845

ENNEKING, --, d of Heinrich Enneking; dom. Strieker farm   1/1845

BRUNE, --, d of Caspar Brune; dom. Woebkenberg farm   1/1845

STUEHRENBERG, --, family (3 adults, 3 cc); dom. ?   6/1845

RESELAGE, --, family farmers (3 cc under 15 years); destina-
    tion New York   5/1848

SCHMID, --, family, with 2 cc under 15 years & 2 cc above 15
    years, farmers; destination New York   5/1848

LINDEMANN, --, farm with w & 3 dd (all dd under 15 years);
    destination New York   5/1848

FRANZLUENING, --, hired hand; took 200 Reichsthaler with him;
    destination Baltimore   1/1848

KLUENENBERG, --, hired hand; destination Baltimore   1/1848

ELKING, --, hired hand; destination Baltimore   1/1848

SCHROEDER, Maria, maid; destination Baltimore   1/1849

RESELAGE, --, d of the Reselage family, no profession; des-
    tination Cincinnati   1/1849

KRUTHAUPT, --, hired hand; took 100 Reichsthaler with him;
    destination Cincinnati   1/1849

Reselage Farming Community (continued)
Sierhausen Partly-owned Farm

KRUTHAUPT, Heinrich, s of farmowner -- Krauthaupt	1/1842
KRUSE, Heinrich, with family; dom. Kruthaupt farm	5/1835
NEDERMANN, Heinrich, with family; dom. Kruthaupt farm	5/1838
RICKING, Bernard Heinrich, with family; dom. Kruthaupt farm	7/1838
RECK, Engel; dom. Meyer farm	1/1836
MEYER, Heinrich; dom. Meyer farm	1/1838
KRUTHAUPT "Little," Josef, brother of farmowner -- "Little" Kurthaupt	1/1831
VON DER HEIDE, Heinrich, with wife; dom. Kurthaupt farm	2/1839
FELDMANN, --, 2 ss of Hermann Feldmann; dom. Wolke Sierhaus cottage	2/1838
TRIMPE "Little", --, sister of farmowner -- "Little" Trimpe	1/1834
MEYER, Hermann, with w & 1 c; dom. Lampe farm	3/1833
STALLO, Heinrich, with family; dom. Lampe farm	9/1841
LAMPE, Friedrich, with family; dom. Lampe farm	8/1843
FELDMANN, --, 2 ss of hired hand -- Feldmann; dom. Lampe farm	2/1837
TRIMPE "Little", --, with family; dom. Lampe farm	5/1835
MEYER, Hermann, with family; dom. Lampe farm	6/1841
DRAHMANN, Bernard, with family; dom. Lampe farm	3/1833
NEDERMANN, Maria; dom. Lampe farm	1/1836
HINNENKAMP, Bernard, with 2 other men; dom. Lampe farm	3/1834
IHLENDORF, Anna Maria, d of houseowner -- Ihlendorf	1/1843

Reselage Farming Community (continued)
Sierhausen Partly-owned Farm

TRIMPE, Josef & Catharina Maria; dom. Trimpen Stelle [place] 2/1834

FRANZLIENING, --, 4 ss of farmowner -- Franzliening 4/1831

FELDMANN, --, family; dom. Wolke Sierhaus [cottage?] 5/1846

MEYER, --, hired hand, with family; dom. Meyer farm 4/1846

KRUTHAUPT "Little," --, cottage owner 7/1846

LINDEMANN, Heinrich; dom. Meyer farm 1/1846

Rottinghausen Farming Community

KRUSE, Josef, s of cottage owner -- Kruse 1/1833

MENKE, --, widow, with family; dom. Kruse cottage 4/1843

FELDMANN, --, ss & d of widow -- Feldmann; dom. "Little" Piening cottage 2/1843

--, Christopher; dom. "Little" Piening cottage 1/1844

HAUSFELD, Josef, with family; dom. Piening farm 3/1838

PARDIEK, Bernard & Engel; dom. Piening farm 2/1834

IGELMANN, Elisabeth; dom. Piening farm 1/1835

ROLFSEN, Bernard, s of widow -- Rolfsen; dom. Piening farm 1/1838

WEHMHOFF, Elisabeth; dom. Piening farm 1/1843

PIENING, --, d of -- Piening; dom. Piening farm? 1/1834

THALE, --, family of; dom. ? 6/1836

--, --, 1 person from farmowner -- Thale's farm 1/1830

--, --, 1 person from farmowner -- Rottinghaus's farm 1/1841

Rottinghausen Farming Community (continued)

--, --, 3 persons from Pellenwessel farm	3/18--
WIETHORN, --, family of widow; dom. Pellenwessel farm	4/1835
HERZOG, --, family of widow; dom. Stuehrenberg farm	3/1844
ROLFSEN, Heinrich; dom. Stuehrenberg farm	1/1841
KRAMER, Anton & Bernd, brothers; dom. Stuehrenberg farm	2/1830
HERZOG, Anna Maria; dom. Stuehrenberg farm	1/1841
ROTTINGHAUS, Christoph; dom. Stuehrenberg farm	1/1841
WUEBKER, Engel & Elise, sisters; dom. with Wolkemeyer	2/1841-1843
ORTMANN, Bernard Heinrich, with w & 1 c; dom. Meyer auf dem Ohrde	3/1833
REHLING, Bernard, with w & 2 cc; dom. Meyer auf dem Ohrde	4/1832
HACKMANN, --, with w; dom. Meyer auf dem Ohrde	2/1844
BUENGER, --, widow, with 3 ss; dom. Meyer auf dem Ohrde	4/1844
BRANDKAMP, Bernard Heinrich; dom. Meyer auf dem Ohrde	1/1841
KORTE, Heinrich; dom. Kohrs Inderrieden	1/18--
WUEBKER, Agnes & Maria, sisters; dom. Kohrs Inderrieden	2/18--
LUEBKE, --, a brother & sister of farmowner -- Luebke; dom. Ossenbeck	2/1839
LUEBKE, --, another brother of the above	1/1842
HENKENBERNS, Gerhard, with family; dom. Luebke farm, Ossenbeck	5/1834
BOEDEKER, Gerhard, with family; dom. Luebke farm, Ossenbeck	8/1833
GOTTBEHOEDE, Heinrich; dom. Luebke farm, Ossenbeck	1/1841
NIEBUR, --, a brother & 2 sisters of farmowner -- Niebur; dom. Ossenbeck	3/1832

Rottinghausen Farming Community (continued)

BRUEGGENSCHMID, --, family; dom. Niebur farm, Ossenbeck	7/1832
BRUEGGENSCHMID? --, daughter	1/1843
GAUSEPOHL, Carl; dom. Gers farm, Ossenbeck	1/1835
RICHTER, Bernard Heinrich; dom. Gers farm, Ossenbeck	3/1833
KRUSE, Heinrich, with family; dom. Gers farm, Ossenbeck	7/1837
NIENABER, --, widow, with family; dom. ?	3/1842
GAUSEPOHL, Josef, with family; dom. Gers farm, Ossenbeck	5/1844
OSSENBECK, Elisabeth; dom. Gers farm, Ossenbeck	1/1844
INDERRIEDEN, Heinrich; dom. Gers farm, Ossenbeck	1/1836
DIEKHAUS, --, widow [with family?]; dom. Herzog farm	5/1843
BERKEMEYER, Georg, with family; dom. Herzog farm	5/1844
MUELLER, --, widow, with family; dom. Herzog farm	3/1844
BRUNE, Maria; dom. Herzog farm	1/1844
GERS UPHAUS, --, 1 brother of farmowner -- Gers Uphaus	1/1837
BORGMANN, --, family; dom. Uphaus farm	6/1842
WITTE, Heinrich, with family; dom. Uphaus farm	8/1843
NIEHAUS, --, s of hired hand -- Niehaus; dom. Tebbemeyer farm	1/1835
MUELLER, Heinrich, with family; dom. Tebbemeyer farm	5/1844
HERZOG, --, widow, with family; dom. Twiessel farm	4/1842
REUTEMANN, Heinrich; dom. Gotting farm	1/1842
KLOENNE, --, hired hand, with family; dom. Meyer farm of. Greven	3/1845
FELDMANN, --, widow, with family; dom. ?	3/1846

Rottinghausen Farming Community (continued)

ENNEKING, Bernd; dom. ?   1/1846

BERTE, --, widow, with family; dom. ?   5/1846

ROLFSEN, --, d of Berend Rolfsen; dom. ?   1/1846

SEEPS, --, d of Berend Seeps; dom. ?   1/1846

THALE, --, d of farmowner -- Thale   1/1846

WESTERHOFF, --, d of houseowner -- Westerhoff; dom. ?   1/1846

WELLMANN, --, farmowner, family of; destination Baltimore   2/1848

FELDMANN, --, hired hand; destination Baltimore   1/1848

STEINEMANN, --, hired hand; destination Baltimore   1/1848

PARDIEK, --, maid; destination Cincinnati   1/1848

WEHMHOFF, --, 1 hired hand & 2 maids, siblings; destination
    Cincinnati   3/1848

PUTTHOFF, --, hired hand; destination Cincinnati   1/1848

BARTELT, --, hired hand; destination Cincinnati   1/1848

WITTROCK, --, brothers, hand laborers; destination Cincin-
    nati   2/1848

WELLMANN, --, hired hand; destination Cincinnati   1/1848

MEYER AUF DEM OHRDE, --, hired hand; destination Cincinnati   1/1849

HERZOG, --, hired hand; destination Cincinnati   1/1849

KOETTER, --, farmowner, with w & 1 c under 15 years; destina-
    tion Baltimore   3/1849

BOEDEKER, --, hired hand; destination Baltimore   1/1849

KRAMER, --, brother & sister, hired hand & maid; destination
    Baltimore   2/1849

Rottinghausen Farming Community (continued)

WUEBKER, --, farmer, with w & 2 cc (1 under 15 years); destination Baltimore   6/1849

BROERMANN, -- ; destination Baltimore   1/1849

STRIEKER, --, hired hand; destination Baltimore   1/1849

SEEP, --, hired hand, with family (with 2 cc under 15 years & 1 c over 15 years); destination Cincinnati   6/1849

PIENING, --, hired hand; destination Cincinnati   1/1849

MOORMANN, --, farmers, brother & sister; destination Cincinnati   2/1849

PELLENWESSEL, --, hired hand; destination Cincinnati   1/1849

BRANDKAMP, --, farmer, with family (3 cc under 15 years); destination Baltimore   7/1849

KRAMER, --, hired hand; destination Baltimore   1/1849

WUEBKER, --, farmer, with family (3 cc under 15 years); destination Baltimore   5/1849

PELLENWESSEL, --, hired hand & maid; destination Baltimore   2/1849

HEIDELMANN, --, hired hand; destination Baltimore   1/1849

REUTEMANN, --; destination Baltimore   1/1849

ENGILBERT, --, farmer, with family (2 ss & 1 d over 15 years); destination Baltimore   5/1849

OSSENBECK, --, hired hand; destination Baltimore   1/1849

ROLFSEN, --, hired hand; destination Baltimore   1/1849

Rueschendorf Farming Community

MEYER, Johann Bernard, with family; dom. Rueschendorf farm   3/1833

DROPPELMANN, Anton, with family; dom. Rueschendorf farm   5/1844

FISCHER, Elisabeth; dom. Rueschendorf farm   1/1843

WILKE-MACKE, Hermann Heinrich, with family; dom. Rueschendorf
    farm   6/1833

OSTERHOFF, Bernard, with family; dom. Rueschendorf farm   2/1836

MEYER, Johann, with family; dom. Kemphues farm   4/1833

PELLENWESSEL, Hermann Heinrich, with family; dom. Kemphues
    farm   7/1834

BAEUMER, Johann Heinrich, with family; dom. Kemphues farm   7/1833

BRINKMANN, Bernard, s of cottage owner -- Brinkmann   1/1841

BORGERDING, Johann Heinrich, with family; dom. Sandermann
    farm   2/1844

MOORMANN, Heinrich; dom. Sandermann farm   1/1844

SANDERMANN "Little," Heinrich, with family; dom. Sandermann
    farm   2/1836

MESCHER, Bernard, with family; dom. Sandermann farm   4/1844

ENNEKING, Bernard, with family; dom. Sandermann farm   8/1844

HEIDKAMP, Hermann Heinrich; dom. with Rusche   1/1844

KERSTING, Johann Bernard, with family; dom. with Rusche   8/1844

BRUNE, Johann Heinrich, with family; dom. with Hakmann   5/1833

BAGGE, Bernard Heinrich, with family; dom. with Hakmann   8/1844

PUTTHOFF, Johann Heinrich, with family; dom. with Hakmann   4/1836

BROKAMP, Bernard, with family; dom. with Hakmann   5/1836

Rueschendorf Farming Community (continued)

BECKMANN, Hermann Heinrich & Engel; dom. with Hakmann	2/1835
TEPE, Catharina; dom. with "Little" Kloenne	1/1842
RONNEBAUM, Heinrich, with family; dom. with "Little" Kloenne	4/1844
BURDIEK, --, widow, with family; dom. with Wernke-Schmiesing	5/1838
BURDIEK, Bernard; dom. with Wernke-Schmiesing	1/1844
PUTTHOFF, Franz Heinrich & Johann Heinrich; dom. Meyer farm	2/1840
RAENKER, Maria Agnes & Elisabeth; dom. Meyer farm	2/1839
MEYER, Johann Heinrich, with family; dom. with Moormann of Kemphausen	4/1844
DECKER, Johann Heinrich, with family; dom. Schwager farm	6/1835
ROEMER, --, widow, with family; dom. Schwager farm	10/1834
SCHWAGER, Heinrich, s of farmowner -- Schwager	1/1832
MACKE, Agnes; dom. Schwager farm	1/1834
GREFER, Franz; dom. Schwager farm	1/1844
ROEMER, Heinrich; dom. with Boerger	1/1832
LANGE, Franz, with family; dom. with Grefer	4/1833
BRINKHOFF, Heinrich, with family; dom. with Grefer	4/1843
RASCHE, Friedrich, with family; dom. with Grefer	4/1844
KRAMER, Johann Heinrich, with family; dom. with Luettmerding	5/1833
KLUENENBERG, Heinrich, with family; dom. with Luettmerding	4/1836
DECKER, Elisabeth; dom. with Luettmerding	1/1841
DOEPKER, Heinrich, with family; dom. with Schmiesing	3/1836
SCHMIESING, Johann Bernard; dom. with Schmiesing	1/1844

Rueschendorf Farming Community (continued)

MOORMANN, Johann Bernard; dom. in the schoolhouse   1/1844

AUSTING, Ferdinand; dom. with Klatte   1/1841

BRINKMANN, Heinrich, with family; dom. with Jasper   5/1839

MACKE, Josef & Heinrich, ss of cottage owner -- Macke of
    Huede   2/1836

FEHRMANN, Bernard, Elisabeth, & Anna Maria, cc of cottage
    owner -- Fehrmann of Huede   3/1836

WEMPE, Franz; dom. with Macke of Hude   1/1836

ELKING, --, widow, with family; dom. with "Big" Kloenne   6/1836

AUF DEM KAMPE, Anna Maria; dom. with "Big" Kloenne   1/1843

SCHUMACHER, Josef; dom. with "Big" Kloenne   1/1844

ARKENBERG, Johann Bernard, with family; dom. with Floettel   6/1836

STANBUSCH, Heinrich, with family; dom. with Floettel   6/1834-1844

RASCHE, Friedrich, Gertrud, & Elisabeth; dom. with
    Floettel   3/1844

WILBERDING, Johann Bernard, cottage owner   1/1834

WILBERDING, --, widow; dom. with Macke of Huede   1/1844

KLEINE, Johann Heinrich, with family; dom. with Ihlendorf   6/1834

MEYER, Hermann Heinrich, with family; dom. with Ihlendorf   5/1839

BOERGER, Hermann, with family; dom. with Wilke-Ihlendorf   2/1844

POEPPELMANN, Johann Heinrich, with family; dom. with Kop-
    hanke   2/1839

BAEUMER, Jakob, with family; dom. with Kophanke   6/1841

WEHMING, --, 3 students; dom. with Kophanke   3/1844

38

Rueschendorf Farming Community (continued)

OSTERHOFF, Bernard & Heinrich; dom. with Kophanke   2/1838

AUSTING, --, widow, with family; dom. Sandermann farm   2/1839

MACKE, Johann Heinrich; dom. Meyer farm   1/1845

HEIDKAMP, Franz, with family; dom. Meyer farm   3/1845

PUTTHOFF, Bernard; dom. Meyer farm   1/1845

STANBUSCH, Heinrich, with family; dom. Floettel farm   3/1845

BAEUMER, Elisabeth; dom. Floettel farm   1/1845

KERSTING, Johann Bernard, with family; dom. with Rusche   8/1845

DOEPKER, Bernard Heinrich, with family; dom. with Rusche   7/1845

BORGERDING, Josef; dom. Sandmann farm   1/1845

BAGGE, Bernard Heinrich, with family; dom. Hakmann farm 6/1845

HEIDKAMP, Josef; dom. Hakmann farm   1/1845

SCHUMACHER, Josef; dom. with "Big" Kloenne [duplicate entry] 1/1845

BURDIEK, Johann Bernard; dom. with Wernke Schmiesing   1/1845

DROEPPELMANN, --, hired hand, with d, his son-in-law B.
    KRAMER & the latter's family (including 2 cc, both
    girls)   6/1845

RASCHE, --, s & 2 dd; dom. Floettel farm   3/1845

BAEUMER, --, hired hand, with family; from Huede   3/1846

ROTTINGHAUS, --, family; dom. ?   5/1846

POHLSCHNEIDER, --, bachelor; dom. ?   1/1846

GREVER, --, widow, with family (4 dd over 15 years); destina-
    tion Baltimore   5/1848

SCHROEDER, Heinrich, hired hand; destination Baltimore   1/1848

Rueschendorf Farming Community (continued)

SCHOENHOEFFT, Bernd, with family (1 c under 15 years)   5/1848

TRENKAMP, Gerd, hired hand; destination Cincinnati   1/1848

MACKE, Elisabeth, maid; destination Cincinnati   1/1848

SCHUMACHER, Agnes, maid; destination Cincinnati   1/1848

Holdorf Community (Gemeinde)
Fladderlohausen Farming Community

DIEKHAUS, Bernd, s of B. Diekhaus; dom. with Gramke in
    Gramke [settlement]   1/1838

UPHAUS, Elisabeth, b REHLING, w of Johann Uphaus (the husband
    "is still here"; dom. with Uphaus in Diekhausen   1/1838

REHLING, Agnes & Engel, orphans from Bokern; dom. Diekhaus in
    Diekhausen   2/1838

BORGMANN, --, widow & landowner, mother w 2 ss; dom. with the
    hereditary lessee of Diekhaus farm in Fladderlohausen   3/1838

BORGMANN, Hermann, s of the above   1/1832

BORGMANN, Gerd, hereditary lessee, with w & 2 cc [additional
    family member not given]; dom. with Diekhaus farm in
    Fladderlohausen   5/1842

VON DER HEIDE, Elisabeth, d of Heinrich von der Heide; dom.
    with Diekhaus   1/1844

VON DER HEIDE, Maria, d of Heinrich von der Heide; dom. with
    Diekhaus   1/1844

UPHAUS, Maria, d of widow -- Uphaus; dom. with Johann of
    Amtern   1/1835

KLAUSING, Heinrich, with w & 1 c; dom. in the household of
    the widow Maria Uphaus   3/1838

MEYER, Berend, with w; dom. with Johann of Amtern   2/1844

Fladderlohausen Farming Community (continued)

LIENESCH, Gertrud, orphan of Heinrich Lienesch; dom. zu Amtern
in Amtern   1/1843

STEINEMANN, --, widow, with 2 cc; dom. with Huelsmann in Fladderlohausen   2/1835

STEINEMANN, Heinrich, s of the above; dom. ?   1/1832

STEINEMANN, Hermann, brother of the above [Heinrich]; dom. ? 1/1833

HAUSFELD, Catharina, d of the late Heinrich Hausfeld; dom.
with Brickwede in Grandorf   1/1833

BRICKWEDE, Hermann Heinrich & Friedrich, ss of widow[er?]
Gerd Brickwede; dom. with Brickwede in Grandorf   2/1844

WANSTROTH, Carl, with w & 4 cc; dom. with Huerkamp in Grandorf   6/1844

ORTMANN, Maria, landowner; dom. with hereditary lessee Herm
Ortmann with Huerkamp   1/1844

TEPEKRUSE, Heinrich, with w & 4 cc; dom. Eschhoffmann farm
in Fladderlohausen   6/1836

DREES, Johann, with w, 2 cc, mother-in-law & her d; dom. with
Eschhoffmann in Fladderlohausen   6/1836

KLAUSING, Bernd, with w & 3 cc; dom. with Eschhoffmann   5/1844

HOENE, Dirk, with w & 2 cc; dom. with Moormann in Amtern4/1833-1835

RENNEKER, Friedrich, with w & 4 cc; dom. Nessmann farm in
Amtern   6/1835

BLAUOHR [blue ear], --, so-called; dom. Nessmann farm in
Amtern   1/1833-1836

BLAUOHR, --, b HOMEYER, w of the above   1/1844

ASSMANN, N. N. [no name?], with w & 1 c, at one time with
Schoenhoefet in Diekhausen   3/1837-1839

REHLING, N. N. [no name?] with w & 3 cc & mother-in-law;
dom. with Siefke in Wahlde   6/1835

Fladderlohausen Farming Community (continued)

TEPE, Hermann Heinrich; dom. Siefke in Wahlde   1/1835

HILGEFORT, Friedrich, landowner, s of widow -- Hilgefort,
    hereditary lessee; dom. Siefke in Wahlde   1/1844

SIEFKE, Elisabeth, d of farm owner -- Siefke in Wahlde   1/1844

MEYER, Catharina, d of Anton Meyer; dom. with Siefke in
    Wahlde   1/1843

MEYER, Gertrud, d of Anton Meyer; dom. with Siefke in Wahlde 1/1844

ZU WAHLDE, Friedrich, with w, 2 ss, daughter-in-law; dom.
    Hinrich zu Wahlde   5/1836

NURRE, --, widow, with 2 cc; dom. with Hinrich zu Wahlde   3/1835

NURRE, Adelheid; dom. ?   1/1838

BROCKMANN, Gerd, with w & 3 cc; dom. with "Big" Kloenne in
    Fladderlohausen   5/1835

POEPPELMANN, Bernard, s of the late -- Poeppelmann; dom. in
    Gramke   1/1833

IHLENDORF, Heinrich; dom. Poeppelmann farm in Gramke   1/1835-1837

SCHOENHOEFT, Bernd, with w; dom. Peoppelmann farm in
    Gramke   2/1836

KENKEL, Catharina, d of widow -- Kenkel, now WULFEKUHL;
    dom. with Huerkamp in Grandorf   1/1844

ORTMANN, Maria, landowner, d of Hermann Ortmann, hereditary
    lessee; dom. with Poeppelmann in Fladderlohausen   1/1844

MEYER, Werner, s of Werner Meyer [Senior?]; dom. with
    Poeppelmann   1/1832

BRINKHUENEFELD, Herm-Hinrich, s of the late cottage owner
    -- Brinkhuenefeld; dom. ?   1/1834

BRINKHUENEFELD, Gerd, s of the late cottage owner -- Brink-
    huenefeld; dom. ?   1/1836-1838

Fladderlohausen Farming Community (continued)

DREES, Herm Heinrich, s of the late Gerd Drees; dom. with Brink-
    huenefeld   1/1833

DREES, Hermann, s of the late Gerd Drees; dom. with Brinkhuene-
    feld   1/1835

DREES, Heinrich & Catharina, siblings of the [two] former emi-
    grants   2/1835

WESSELING, Heinrich, s of Bernd Wesseling; dom. with Grote in
    Fladderlohausen   1/1835

WITTERIEDE, Catharina, d of cottage owner -- Witteriede in
    Grandorf   1/1844

WIETE, Heinrich, with w; dom. with "Big" Grimme in Grandorf 2/1843

WOLKEHANEKAMP, --, cottage owner, with w & 2 cc; dom. in Flad-
    derlohausen (Bernd Tepekruse bought the cottage)   5/1834-1836

NOLTE, Gerd, s of the late Christian Nolte; dom. with Wolke-
    hanekamp   1/1834

SCHULTE, Catharina, d of Heinrich Schulte; dom. with Frye,
    Fladderlohausen   1/1834

SCHULTE, Heinrich, brother of the above; dom. ?   1/1835-1837

SCHULTE, Herm Hinrich, brother of the above; dom. ?   1/1844

FRYE, Gerd, s of cottage owner -- Frye (deceased); dom. Flad-
    derlohausen   1/1835

UPHAUS, Gerd, with w & 1 c; dom. with Frye, Fladderlohausen 3/1835

THESE, Heinrich, s of the late Gerd "Big" These; dom. ?   1/1833

THESE, Herm Hinrich, brother of the above; dom. ?   1/1834

THESE, Herm, brother of the above; dom. ?   1/1838

THESE, Adelheid, sister of the above; dom. ?   1/1844

LIENING, Heinrich, s of cottage owner -- Liening; dom. Flad-
    derlohausen   1/1844

Fladderlohausen Farming Community (continued)

BARLAGE, --, with s, daughter-in-law, & 1 c; dom. with cottage
owner -- Kleine in Fladderlohausen   4/1835

SCHULTE, --, widow of Friedrich Schulte, with 2 dd; dom. with
cottage owner -- Kleine in Fladderlohausen   3/1841

SCHULTE, Heinrich, with w & 1 c; dom. Kleine cottage   3/1838

KORTE, Catharina, d of B. Hinrich Korte; dom. Kleine cottage 1/1838

KORTE, Maria, sister of the above; dom. ?   1/1841

KURRE, Hermann Heinrich, s of the present widow -- Kurre; dom.
Kleine cottage   1/1841

MACKETEPE, Elisabeth, d of the late cottage owner -- Macketepe, Fladderlohausen   1/1833

MACKETEPE, Maria, sister of the above; dom. ?   1/1835

MACKETEPE, Bernard, brother of the above; dom. ?   1/1838

DETMER, Caspar, with w & 2 cc; dom. Macketepe [cottage?] 4/1841

DETMER, Berend, s of the above; dom. ?   1/1837

DETMER, Josef, brother of the above [Berend?]; dom. ?   1/1838-1840

MEYER, Elisabeth, d of widow -- Meyer; dom. with Macketepe 1/1844

NIENABER, Hermann, s of cottage owner -- Nienaber, Fladderlohausen   1/1839-1840

BOJE, Heinrich, s of the late Gerd Boje; dom. with Nienaber
1/1835-1837

BOJE, Gerd, brother of the above; dom. ?   1/1836-1838

BOJE, Elisabeth, sister of the above; dom. ?   1/1836-1838

MOORMANN, Berend, s of cottage owner -- Moormann, Fladderlohausen   1/1834

VOELKERDING, Adelheid, d of Johann Voelkerding; dom. with
"Little" Moormann in Fladderlohausen   1/1835

Fladderlohausen Farming Community (continued)

VOELKERDING, Johann, with w & 2 cc; dom. with "Little" Moormann 4/1837

VOELKERDING, Bernard, s of the above; dom. ? 1/1836

WOBBELER, Berend, with w, 1 c, & mother; dom. with cottage
owner Drees, Fladderlohausen. 4/1834

WOBBELER, Johann, brother of the above; dom. ? 1/1832

DREES, Friedrich, s of widow -- Drees; dom. with Drees, Fladderlohausen 1/1843

GAUSEPOHL, Herm Heinrich, s of Herm Gausepohl; dom. with Drees
[Fladderlohausen] 1/1834

MACKE-KRUSE, Arnd, brother of cottage owner -- Macke-Kruse,
Fladderlohausen 1/1833

KRUSE, Catharina, d of cottage owner -- Macke-Kruse, Fladderlohausen 1/1844

KRUSE, Hermann Heinrich, with w; dom. with cottage owner Macke-
Kruse 2/1835

TRIMPE, --, widow, with son-in-law, 2 dd, & 1 c; dom. most
recently with -- Kruse 5/1844

TRIMPE, Heinrich, s of the above; dom. ? 1/1834

TRIMPE, Herm & Gerd, ss of the above; dom. ? 2/1836-1838

BOJE, Catharina, sister of cottage owner -- Boje 1/1838-1840

WOBBELER, Maria & Catharina, dd of the late cottage owner
-- Wobbeler in Fladderlohausen 2/1844

WANSTROTH, Heinrich, s of widow -- Wanstroth; dom. with
Wobbeler 1/1844

SEEPS, Bernard Heinrich & Josef, ss of the late cottage
owner (Berend) Seeps 2/1836

BROCKMANN, Heinrich, with w & 3 cc; dom. with cottage owner
-- Bloemker in Fladderlohausen 5/1834

Fladderlohausen Farming Community (continued)

KLOENNE "Little", Catharina, d of cottage owner -- "Little"
Kloenne, Fladderlohausen   1/1844

SCHULTE, Heinrich, s of former farm owner -- Schulte, Fladderlohausen   1/1844

FENNEMANN, Gerd, brother of cottage owner -- Fennemann, Fladderlohausen   1/1834

FENNEMANN, Herm & Elisabeth, sisters of the above; dom. Fladderlohausen   2/1836

FENNEMANN, Heinrich, s of cottage owner -- Fennemann, Fladderlohausen   1/1844

WIENHOLD, Herm Heinrich; dom. with Vogel, Fladderlohausen (his
w & 2 cc remain here)   1/1834

HOEGEMANN, Maria, d of cottage owner -- Hoegemann, Fladderlohausen   1/1841

SCHULTE *sive* [formerly?] HUETTEMANN, Heinrich, with w & 2 cc
& brother; dom. Huettemann cottage (which was bought by
-- Nienaber)   5/1844

FENNEMANN, Herm Heinrich, brother of cottage owner -- Fennemann, Fladderlohausen   1/1837

GAUSEPOHL, Adelheid, owner of Gausepohl cottage, with 2 dd
(the cottage was bought by Gerd Frye)   3/1834

WANSTROTH "Little," Elisabeth, sister of the present cottage
owner -- [Wanstroth?], Fladderlohausen   1/1844

WANSTROTH "Little," Heinrich, brother of the present cottage
owner -- [Wanstroth?], Fladderlohausen   1/1833

WANSTROTH "Little," Herm Heinrich, brother of the present cottage owner -- [Wanstroth?], Fladderlohausen   1/1835

SCHULTE, Margaretha, d of the late -- Schulte; dom. with
Tabehuenefeld   1/1841

SCHULTE, Hermann & Heinrich, ss of the late -- Schulte; dom.
with Tabehuenefeld   2/1844

46

Fladderlohausen Farming Community (continued)

SCHULTE, Bernd, owner of half of Tabehuenefeld, with w & 4 cc
   (the other half belongs to Friedrich WITTERIEDE)   6/1844

GRAMANN, Elisabeth, d of widow -- Gramann; dom. with Wesseling   1/1844

STELTENPOHL "Little," Heinrich, s of cottage owner -- "Little"
   Steltenpohl, Fladderlohausen   1/1833

WESSELING, Johann, "new" farmer, with w & 4 cc (bought out by
   -- "Little HANEKAMP)   6/1838

WESSELING, Herm Hinrich, s of the above; dom. ?   1/1833

WESSELING, Johann & Maria, cc of "new' farmer -- Wesseling
   [the above-mentioned?]   2/1835

GAUSEPOHL, Friedrich, "new" farmer, with w & 3 cc (bought out
   by -- IN DER RIEDEN)   6/1844

GAUSEPOHL, Gerd, "new" farmer, with 5 cc (position now owned
   by -- FENNEMANN)   5/1836

SCHULTE, Heinrich, brother of innkeeper & "new" farmer Herm
   Heinrich Schulte   1/1835

SCHULTE, Bernardina, sister of the above   1/1844

SEEPS, "Little," Herm Hinrich, s of "new" farmer Henrich
   "Little" Seeps   1/1841

STUNTEBECK, Berend, family of; Catholic   3/1845

KRUSE, Arend, family of; Catholic   4/1845

KORTE, Friedrich, family of; Catholic   4/1845

KORTE, Berend, family of; Catholic   2/1845

URLAGE, Heinrich, family of; Catholic   7/1845

WESSELING, Heinrich, family of; Catholic   5/1845

DUERSTOCK, Berend; Catholic   1/1845

Fladderlohausen Farming Community (continued)

BECKMANN, Elisabeth; Catholic	1/1845
KURRE, Heinrich; Catholic	1/1845
GRAMANN, Josef; Catholic	1/1845
KRUSE, Margaretha; Catholic	1/1845
SCHULTE, Maria; Catholic	1/1845
VON DER HEIDE, Catharina; Catholic	1/1845
POEPPELMANN, Catharina; Catholic	1/1845
HILGEFORT, Elisabeth; Catholic	1/1845
ORTMANN, Elisabeth; Catholic	1/1845
NURRE, Berend; Catholic	1/1845
WESSELING, Elisabeth; Catholic	1/1845
BLOEMER, Josef; Catholic	1/1845
BORGMANN, Heinrich; Catholic	1/1845
KLOENNE "Little," --, widow, with family; Protestant	6/1845
FENNEMANN, Elise; Protestant	1/1845
MOORMANN, Catharina; Protestant	1/1845
HANEKAMP "Little," Hermann Heinrich; Protestant	1/1845
SEEP "Little," Gerd; Protestant	1/1845
WOLKEHANEKAMP, Hermann Heinrich; Protestant	1/1845
KLEIBOECKER, Friedrich; Protestant	1/1845
BRICKWEDE, Heinrich; Protestant	1/1845
WOLKEHANEKAMP, Gerd; Protestant	1/1845

Fladderlohausen Farming Community (continued)

LIENSCH, --, widow, with family	3/1846
GIERE, Elisabeth, maid	1/1846
KRUSE, Elisabeth, maid	1/1846
GAUSEPOHL, Heinrich, tailor	1/1846
FRYE, --, widow, with 1 d over 15 years, peasants, no property; took 150 Reichsthaler with them	2/1846
SCHULTE, Heinrich, with [w?], 1 s & 2 dd (all 3 cc under 15 years); peasants, no property	5/1846
LIENESCH, --, widow, with 2 dd (over 15 years; 1 d is a maid); peasants, no property	3/1846
STALLO, Franz, hired hand	1/1846
BOECKMANN, Gerd, hired hand	1/1846
THESE, Josef, carpenter	1/1846
LONNEMANN, Catharina, maid	1/1846
VENNEMANN, Heinrich, hired hand	1/1846
KNOLLENBERG, Friedrich, hired hand	1/1846
KLEIBOECKER, Johann Heinrich, hired hand	1/1847
RENNEKER, Johann Heinrich, hired hand	1/1847
MOORMANN, Josef, schoolteacher; took 50 Reichsthaler with him	1.1847
NURRE, Heinrich, tailor	1/1847
NURRE, Maria, maid	1/1847
GAUSEPOHL, Elisabeth, maid	1/1847
POEPPELMANN, Henrich, hired hand	1/1847

Fladderlohausen Farming Community (continued)

LIENING, Elisabeth, no profession   1/1847

SCHOENHOEFT, Maria, maid   1/1847

FELDMANN, Heinrich, with [w?] & s (over 15 years), peasants,
    no property; took 1300 Reichsthaler with them   3/1847

HILGEFORT, --, widow, with 2 cc (1 under 15 years), peasants,
    no property   3/1847

MOORMANN, Heinrich, with [w?] & 3 cc (1 under 15 years),
    peasants, no property   5/1847

HEMPELER, Caroline, maid   1/1847

ROEWE, Elisabeth, maid   1/1847

FRYE, Heinrich, hired hand   1/1848

HUENEFELD, Caroline, maid   1/1848

GIERE, Catharina, maid   1/1848

MEYER, Hermann Heinrich, hired hand   1/1848

WOBBELER, Adelheid, maid   1/1848

MEYER, --, widow of Arnd Meyer, with 1 s & 3 dd (all over 15
    years), peasants from Wahlde   5/1849

MACKE, Elisabeth, maid from Grandorf   1/1849

INDERRIEDEN, Maria, maid from Grandorf   1/1849

BECKMANN, Heinrich, hired hand from Fladderlohausen   1/1849

WULFEKUHLE, Heinrich, hired hand from Fladderlohausen   1/1849

ESCHEN, Heinrich, hired hand from Fladderlohausen   1/1849

HAUSFELD, Heinrich, musician from Fladderlohausen   1/1849

HAUSFELD, Catharina, maid from Fladderlohausen   1/1849

Fladderlohausen Farming Community (continued)

MEYER, Catharina, maid from Fladderlohausen   1/1849

GIER, Bernardine, maid from Fladderlohausen   1/1849

KNOLLENBERG, Gerd, hired hand from Fladderlohausen   1/1849

SEEP "Little," Catharina, maid from Fladderlohausen; took
100 Reichsthaler with her   1/1849

SEEP "Little," Maria, maid from Fladderlohausen; took 100
Reichsthaler with her   1/1849

HEMPELMANN, Gerd, hired hand from Fladderlohausen   1/1849

MEYER, Maria, milliner [Putzmacherin] from Grandorf   1/1849

MEYER, Bernardine, milliner from Grandorf   1/1849

Holdorf Farming Community

HAVERKAMP, Hermann Henrich, with family; dom. with Boelling
in Holdorf   4/1832

SCHULTE, Heinrich, with family; dom. with Timpermann in Hol-
dorf   2/1832

MOORMANN, Hermann Henrich, with family; dom. with Lampe-Goess-
ling in Holdorf   5/1832

VON HANDORFF, Bernd; dom. with Lampe-Goessling in Holdorf   1/1832

STRUCKHOFF, Heinrich; dom. with Struckhoff in Holdorf   1/1833

DIEKHAUS, Heinrich, with family; dom. with Neteler in Hol-
dorf   4/1833

KOOPMANN, --, s & 3 dd of -- Koopmann; dom. with Neteler in
Holdorf   4/1833

BERTE, Heinrich, cottage owner?; dom. with Berte in Holdorf   4/1833

BERTE, Josef, s of cottage owner -- Berte in Holdorf   1/1833

Holdorf Farming Community (continued)

HOERSTMANN, --, s & 2 dd of "new" farmer -- Hoerstmann in
Holdorf   3/1833

STRUNK, Hermann, with family; dom. with Stahtmann in Holdorf 4/1833

JAKOBS, Gerd, farm owner, with family; dom. in Holdorf   5/1833

ORTMANN, Wilhelm, with family; dom. with Tepe-Ortmann in Holdorf   4/1833

SCHLARMANN, Junker [given name? or class title?], cottage
owner, with family; dom. in Holdorf   6/1833

SCHLARMANN, Junker, former farm owner, with family; dom. in
Holdorf   3/1833

LIENING, Bernard Heinrich, with family; dom. with Wernken in
Handorf   10/1833

LIENING, Heinrich, with family; dom. with Nienkroeger in Handorf   3/1833

HENKENBEHRENS, Heinrich; dom. with Wernken in Handorf   1/1833

KRAMER, Bernd; dom. with Arens in Handorf   1/1833

HILLE-ORTMANN, --, cottage owner, with family; dom. in Holdorf   6/1834

TIMPERMANN, --, 2 dd [of -- Timpermann]; dom. with Boelling
in Holdorf   1/1834

WEHRY, Catharina & Bernd; dom. with Boelling in Holdorf   2/1834

BEI DER HAKE, Friedrich; dom. with Annen in Handorf   1/1834

ANNEN, Friedrich, s of farm owner -- Annen in Handorf   1/1835

ANNEN, Margaretha & Dorothea; dom. with Annen in Handorf   2/1835

DECKER, --, widow, with family; dom. with Hellbusch in Handorf   3/1835

BOECKMANN, Heinrich, with family; dom. with Borgmann in Handorf   7/1836

Holdorf Farming Community (continued)

DUERSTOCK, Bernd, with family; dom. with Arens in Handorf   5/1836

SIEFKE, --, cottage owner, with family; dom. in Handorf   7/1836

KESSING, Bernd, with family; dom. with Kessing in Handorf   7/1836

TEPE, Bernd, with family; dom. with Wernken in Handorf   3/1836

TEPE, Hermann Heinrich; dom. with Wernken in Handorf   1/1836

HOERSTMANN, --, cottage owner with family; dom. in Holdorf   7/1838

MEYER, Franz, with family; dom. with Lampe-Goessling in Holdorf   8/1838

MEYER, Gerhard, s of "new" farmer [-- Meyer]; dom. with Lampe-Goessling in Holdorf   1/1838

SCHROEDER, --, d of cottage owner -- Schroeder in Holdorf   1/1838

STRUCKHOFF, Catharina; dom. with Wille-Ortmann in Holdorf   1/1838

BORGMANN, Bernd, with family; dom. with Luthmer in Holdorf   5/1838

GOSMANN, Henrich, with family; dom. with Druehe in Holdorf   3/1838

LIENING, Bernd, with family; dom. at the windmill in Holdorf   9/1838

STRATHMANN, --, farm owner, with family; dom. in Holdorf   7/1838

STRUCKHOFF, Heinrich; dom. with Struckhoff in Holdorf   1/1838

JOHANNING, Heinrich; dom. with Johanning in Holdorf   1/1838

PILLE, Heinrich; dom. with Struckhoff in Holdorf   1/1838

GOSMANN, --, 2 cc of former farm owner -- Gosmann in Holdorf 2/1838

UPHAUS, Wilhelm, cottage owner, with family; dom. in Holdorf 6/1838

STALL, Franz, with family; dom. with Boelling in Holdorf   5/1838

DRUEHE, W., cottage owner, with family; dom. with Metten-Tepe in Holdorf   5/1838

53

Holdorf Farming Community (continued)

LAMPE-GOESSLING, --, farm owner, with family; dom. in Holdorf   3/1838

PILLE, Maria; dom. with Haverkamp in Holdorf   1/1838

HOLLENBECK, Elisabeth; dom. with Haverkamp in Holdorf   1/1838

KURRE, Hermann Heinrich; dom. with Tepe-Ortmann in Holdorf   1/1838

BERTE, --, siblings; dom. with Meyer in Holdorf   2/1838

PRIESHOF, Heinrich, with family; dom. with Junker Schlarman in Holdorf   3/1838

SCHLARMANN, Josef; s of "new" farmer [-- Schlarmann] in Holdorf   1/1838

ORTMANN, Herm Heinrich, with family; dom. with "Big" Schlarmann in Holdorf   4/1838

BRINKHOFFMANN (HEILSCHE), --, with family; dom. with Brinkmann in Holdorf   4/1838

NURRE or METTEN, --, with family; dom. with Metten-Tepe in Holdorf   4/1838

SCHLARMANN, Johann; s of farm owner [-- Schlarmann]   1/1838

HERBST, Elisabeth; dom. with Haverkamp   1/1838

HAVERKAMP, Elisabeth, d of deacon [*Kuester*] -- Haverkamp; dom. in Holdorf   1/1839

STRUCKHOFF, Heinrich, with family; dom. with Boelling in Holdorf   9/1839

VOELKERDING, Arnd, with family; dom. with Struckhoff in Holdorf   4/1839

VOELKERDING, --, s of cottage owner -- Voelkerding in Holdorf   1/1839

AUFM OHRDE, --, s of cottage owner -- Aufm Ohrde in Holdorf   1/1839

Holdorf Farming Community (continued)

WUEBKE, Elisabeth; dom. with Schroeder in Holdorf	1/1839
SCHROEDER, --, d of cottage owner -- Schroeder in Holdorf	1/1839
OEKE, Elisabeth; dom with "Little" Schlarmann in Holdorf	1/1839
HILLE ORTMANN, --, d of cottage owner -- Hille Ortmann in Holdorf	1/1839
MEYER, Johann; dom. with Johanning in Holdorf	1/1840
HOLLENBECK, --, with family; dom. with Haverkamp in Holdorf	4/1840
IM DIEKE, B., married woman; dom. with Haverkamp in Holdorf	1/1841
KLAUSING, Bernd, "new" farmer in Holdorf	1/1844
OEKE, Heinrich; dom. with "Little" Schlarmann in Holdorf	1/1844
DETMER, Lukas, with family; dom. with Boelling in Holdorf	4/1844
SCHLARMANN, Hermann Heinrich, "new" farmer, with family; dom. in Holdorf	2/1844
BERTE, Josef; dom. with Boelling in Holdorf	1/1844
URLAGE, Margaretha; dom. with Lampe-Goessling in Holdorf	1/1844
HELLEBUSCH, Franz, farm owner, with family; dom. in Handorf	11/1844
HONKOMP [so spelled], Heinrich, with family; dom. with Helebusch in Handorf	7/1844
WEHLAGE, Heinrich, with family; dom. with Nienkroeger in Handorf	7/1844
STAGGENBORG, Elisabeth; dom. with Arens in Handorf	1/1844
NIEHAUS, Elisabeth; dom. with Arens in Handorf	1/1844
VON HANDORF, Elisabeth; dom. with Borgmann in Handorf	1/1844
WOERMANN, Elisabeth; dom. with Borgmann in Handorf	1/1844

Holdorf Farming Community (continued)

WOERMANN, Anna Maria; dom. with Borgmann in Handorf   1/1844

HILLE ORTMANN, Herm, with family; dom. with Voelkerding in
    Holdorf   4/1844

MACKE, Henrich, with family; dom. with Siefken in Handorf   4/1844

LINNEMANN, Hermann Heinrich; dom. with Hellebusch in Handorf 1/1844

SCHOENHOEFT, Friedrich; dom. with Hellebusch in Handorf   1/1844

HUELSMANN, Bernd; dom. with Annen in Handorf   1/1844

TIMPERMANN, Heinrich, cottage owner, with family   7/1845

WEHRY, --, widow, with family   3/1845

URLAGE, Catharina   1/1845

ASBREHE, Margaretha   1/1845

GOSMANN, Elisabeth   1/1845

TIMPERMANN, Henrich   1/1845

OSTERHUES, Anna   1/1845

FELDMANN, Anna, lady's companion [*Haustochter*]   1/1845

KLAUSING, Clemens, watchmaker; took 50 Reichsthaler with him 1/1846

WUEBKER, --, widow   3/1846

STRUCKHOFF, --, widow of Gerd Struckhoff, with 4 cc over
    15 years (2 male & 3 female persons--1 hired hand &
    1 maid); not property owners; took 220 Reichsthaler
    with them   5/1846

STRATEGIER, Hermann Heinrich, with [w?], s & d (both under
    15 years), not a property owner, shoe repairman   4/1846

WIBKE, Heinrich, with family (s under 15 years), peasants,
    not a property owner   4/1846

Holdorf Farming Community (continued)

URLAGE, Arnd, hired hand   1/1846

STRUCKHOFF, Bernd, hired hand   1/1846

PILLE, Bernd, hired hand   1/1846

PILLE, Hermann, carpenter   1/1846

VON HANDORF, Heinrich, peasant   1/1846

TEPE-ORTMANN, Catharina, farm owner   1/1846

BERTE, Bernard, cabinetmaker   1/1846

FELDMANN, Hermann Heinrich, hired hand   1/1847

OSTERHUES, Johann Heinrich, hired hand   1/1847 .

ORTMANN, Hermann Heinrich, carpenter   1/1847

BERTE, Johann, cabinetmaker, with family (1 c over 15 years),
    not a property owner; took 900 Reichsthaler with them
    (mother & son)   [This entry seems wrong.]   2/1847

STRUCKHOFF, Werner, peasant, with [w?] & 2 cc (1 c under
    15 years), not a property owner; took 80 Reichsthaler
    with them   4/1847

ORTMANN, --, widow of Heinrich Ortman, with 3 cc (1 c under
    15 years; 1 d a maid) not a property owner   4/1847

METTE, Hermann Heinrich, peasant, with [w?] & 1 s & 3 dd
    (3 cc under 15 years); took 800 Reichsthaler with them   6/1847

VOELKERDING, Hermann, peasant, with family, not property
    owner; took 700 Reichsthaler with them   2/1847

GOESSLING, --, widow of Arnd Goessling, peasant, with s
    (over 15 years), not property owners; took 200 Reichs-
    thaler with them   2/1847

BARLAGE, Bernardine, maid   1/1847

POELKING, Maria Anna, maid   1/1847

Holdorf Farming Community (continued)

WEHRY, Henrich, hired hand   1/1847

DETMER, Maria, no profession   1/1847

HAVERKAMP, Bernardina; took 50 Reichsthaler with her   1/1847

SUEDKAMP, Heinrich, hired hand   1/1847

MEYER, --, widow of Hermann Heinrich Meyer, with d (under 15
    years), day laborer, no property   2/1848

NEUS, --, widow of Heinrich Neus, day laborer, with d (under
    15 years), no property   2/1848

TIMPERMANN, Heinrich, with [w?] & 3 cc (1 c under 15 years);
    took 110 Reichsthaler with them; 2 sons were hired men   5/1848

EKELMANN, Heinrich, hired hand from Handorf   1/1848

EKELMANN, Bernard, hired hand from Handorf   1/1848

POELKING, Johann, peasant, with [w?] & 2 cc (both under 15
    years); took 110 Reichsthaler with them   4/1849

GIERE, --, widow of Hermann Heinrich Giere, peasant, with 3
    cc (1 c under 15 years); took 150 Reichsthaler with her   3/1849

NIEHUES, --, widow of Heinrich Niehues, with 3 ss & 2 dd
    (1 c under 15 years); 2 dd were maids; 2 persons went
    to Holland   6/1849

WEHRY, Bernd, peasant, day laborer & night watchman, with s
    (over 15 years)   2/1849

HAVERKAMP, Bernardine, maid   1/1849

JOHANNING, Hermann Heinrich; went to Holland   1/1849

MOORMANN BEIM VORDE, Bernd, hired hand   1/1849

SUDING, Franz, day laborer   1/1849

PILLE, Hermann Heinrich, hired hand   1/1849

FERNEDING, Elisabeth, maid   1/1849

58

Ihorst Farming Community

KLAUSING, Bernd, s of Bernd Klausing; dom. Borgerding farm 1/1831

BARHORST, Franz, s of farm owner -- Barhorst 1/1832

FERNEDING, Josef, s of farm owner -- Ferneding 1/1832

BARHORST, Hermann Heinrich, s of farm owner -- Barhorst 1/1833

SCHWEGMANN, Josef, s of Heinrich Schwegmann in der Hovesaat 1/1833

HAVERKAMP, Carl, with family 6/1833

FERNEDING, Catharina, d of farm owner -- Ferneding 1/1833

PRIESHOFF, Heinrich, with family; dom. Heidlage farm 3/1833

JOHANNING, Bernd & Gerd, ss of Bernd Johanning; dom. ? 2/1833

HERMES, Christopher, s of Carl Hermes; dom. Ferneding farm 1/1834

BORGERDING, Heinrich, with family; dom. Ferneding farm 5/1834

DORTMANN, Adelheid, d of Bernd Dortmann; dom. with Wehebrink 1/1835

GREFENSTETTE, Elisabeth, d of H. Grefenstette; dom. with
    Otto Grefenstette 1/1836

WOLKING, Heinrich, with family; from the Hovesaat 6/1838

SCHROEDER, Margaretha, d of Anton Schroeder; dom. Hovesaat 1/1838

GREFENSTETTE, Dorothea & Carl, cc of Carl Grefenstette; dom.
    Hovestaat 2/1838

SCHWEGMANN, Heinrich, with family; dom. Borgerding farm 5/1838

KRUSE, Franz Heinrich, s of Gerd Kruse; dom. Borgerding farm 1/1838

DON LEHMDEN, Margaretha, d of Wessel von Lehmden; dom. Ferne-
    ding farm 1/1838

STRUCKHOFF, Bernd, with family; dom. Barhorst farm 4/1838

SCHROEDER, Franz & Carl, ss of Heinrich Schroeder; dom.
    Ferneding farm 2/1838

Ihorst Farming Community (continued)

STRUNK, --, widow, with family; dom. Barhorst farm   5/1838

FANGMANN, Johann Heinrich, s of Heinrich Fangmann; dom. Bar-
    horst farm   1/1838

MIDDENDORF, Bernd, s of Heinrich Middendorf; dom. with Wehe-
    brink   1/1838

WEHEBRINK, Herm, s of Lukas Wehebrink; dom. with Wehebrink   1/1838

STRUCKHOFF, Carl, s of Herm Struckhoff; dom. with Ferneding   1/1839

HERMES, Carl; dom. with Ferneding   1/1839

BLOEMER, Hermann Heinrich, s of H. H. Bloemer; dom. with
    Ferneding   1/1840

GREFENSTETTE, Josef & Arnold, ss of Carl Grefenstette; dom.
    Hovesaat   2/1841

SCHROEDER, Anton, with family; dom. Hovesaat   5/1841

BARLAGE, Heinrich, with family; dom. Hovesaat   9/1841

RUHOLL, --, with family; dom. Hovesaat   3/1841

HINXLAGE, Dina, d of Gerd Hinxlage; dom. with Nienhaus   1/1841

MIDDENDORF, Catharina, d of Heinrich Middendorf; dom. with
    Wehebrink   1/1841

ORTMANN, Josef, s of Herm Heinrich Ortmann; dom. with Ferne-
    ding   1/1842

MIDDENDORF, Henrich Arnd, with family; from the Hovesaat   4/1843

GREFENSTETTE, Carl, with family; from the Hovesaat   4/1843

SCHWEENS, Elisabeth, d of Fritz Schweens; dom. Hovesaat   1/1843

VON DER HEIDE, Gerde, with family; from the Hovesaat   7/1844

KRUSE, Josefine, d of Gerd Kruse; dom. with Borgerding   1/1844

Ihorst Farming Community (continued)

VON LEHMDEN, Henrich Arnd, s of Wessel von Lehmden; dom. with
    Ferneding   1/1844

SCHROEDER, Catharina, d of Heinrich Schroeder; dom. with
    Ferneding   1/1844

HINXLAGE, Johann & Elisabeth, cc of Gerd Hinxlage; dom. Nien-
    haus   2/1844

MEYER, Carl Anton, with family; dom. with Ferneding
    (30 May 1845)   4/1845

BORGERDING, --, widow, with family; dom. formerly with Weller-
    ding, now with Kloecker   (30 March 1845)   4/1845

ORTMANN, Herm Heinrich, "he set himself free" [from military
    service?]; dom. with Ferneding (30 May 1845)   1/1845

BLOEMER, Franz, "he is in the Reserve" [military?]; dom. with
    Ferneding (30 May 1845)   1/1845

VON LEHMDEN, Catharina; dom. with Ferneding (1 October)   1/1845

TRENKAMP, Wilhelm, with d; dom. in the Hovesaat (1 October) 2/1845

DORTMANN, Bernd, "he did not free himself [from military ser-
    vice?]"; dom. with Borgerding (1 October)   1/1845

MEYER, Margarethe; dom. Sieve farm (1 October)   1/1845

HOLBROCK, Catharina; dom. from the Hovesaat (1 October)   1/1845

BLOEMER, Bernardina; dom. Ferneding farm (15 October)   1/1845

SCHWEENS, Dina & Catharina, dd of Anton Schweens; dom.
    Hovesaat (15 October)   2/1845

VON DER HEIDE, Hermann, "he set himself free" [from military
    service?]; dom. Hovesaat (1 November)   1/1845

BARHORST, Catharina   1/1846

HASKAMP, Ferdinand   1/1846

SCHROEDER, Catharina   1/1846

Ihorst Farming Community (continued)

BROKMANN (BECKMANN), --, hired hand, with family   3/1846

BRAMLAGE, Heinrich, with family (1 s under 15 years),
    peasants, no property (11 August)   3/1846

HASKAMP, Ferdinand, peasant in the Hovesaat; took 50 Reichs-
    thaler with him (11 August)   1/1846

BARHORST, Catharina, land owner, d of farm owner -- Barhorst
    (11 August)   1/1846

SCHERDER, Anton, peasant; he emigrates alone, his wife Anton-
    ette Scherder, b WIEGEL, remains here for a while with
    1 c (11 August)   1/1846

HINXLAGE, Gerd, with family (1 s under 15 years); not a prop-
    erty owner; from Neuhaus Wiese (15 September)   3/1846

SIEVE, Carolina, d of farm owner -- Sieve   1/1846

BLOEMER, --, married woman, with s & d under 15 years, to
    join her husband (father of the children) who emigrated
    to America 2 years ago; not property owners   3/1846

MIDDENDORF, Johann Heinrich, hired hand   1/1847

SCHWEENS, Heinrich, hired hand   1/1847

BLOEMER, --, widow, peasant, with 2 cc over 15 years; not
    property owner   3/1848

SCHWEER, Josef, hired hand   1/1848

KRUSE, Josef, hired hand   1/1848

ORTMANN, Bernd, with wife; not property owner   2/1848

VON DER HEIDE, Heinrich, hired hand   1/1848

KRUSE, Hermann, hired hand   1/1849

VON DER HEIDE, Hermann, hired hand   1/1849

WOBBELER, Catharina, widow; emigrated alone   1/1849

Ihorst Farming Community (continued)

SCHNECKER, Josef, peasant, with w & 1 c under 15 years; not property owner	3/1849
SCHERDER, Antonette, emigrates to join her husband	1/1849
MUEGGENBORG, Heinrich, hired hand	1/1849
HOFMANN, Marianne, maid	1/1849

N.B.: The emigrating hired hands are doing so to avoid military service. The emigrating maids are seeking marriage partners.

Neuenkirchen Community [Gemeinde]

Bieste Farming Community

PLAGGE, Bernd, brother of farm owner -- Plagge	1/1833
BOEKE, Bernd, & his half-sister Marianne LONNEMANN, messenger	2/1834
WEBER, Bernard Heinrich, "new" farmer, with w & c	3/1835
WESTENDORF, Josef, hired hand; dom. Kuebbing farm	1/1835
TEBBE-BIDENHARN, Bernard, brother of farm owner -- Tebbe-Bidenharn	1/1836
KNABKE, --, widow, maid, with 4 cc; dom. Kuebbing farm	5/1836
TRIMPE, Diedrich, hired hand	1/1836
STEINKAMP, Johann Heinrich, hired hand	1/1832
THIEMANN, Elisabeth, maid	1/1839
GREVE, Catharina, Gertrud, Elisabeth, & Josef, cc of Bernard Heinrich Greve	4/1840
HUELSMANN, Elisabeth, maid	1/1840
BUESCHER, Heinrich, hired hand	1/1842

Bieste Farming Community (continued)

MIDDENDORF, Bernard, brother of farm owner -- Middendorf   1/1843

MUEESMANN, Friedrich & Gerhard, hired hands   2/1843

MAESCHER, Heinrich & Gertrud, messenger   2/1843

WIEGHAUS, Bernard & Maria, messenger   2/1843

POHLMANN, Diedrich, with w & 7 cc; dom. with Schwietering   9/1844

PRUES, Bernard, Heinrich, Josef, Gertrud, & Elisabeth, siblings, all unmarried--regarded as a family   5/1844

BOEDEKER, Bernard, s of farmowner -- Boedeker   1/1844

SPECKBAUCH, Josef, Grethmarie, & Anna Maria, cc of farm
 owner -- Speckbauch   3/1844

SCHNEIDHORST, Friedrich, hired hand at Gosekuhle farm   1/1844

STICKFORT, --, d of farmowner -- Stickfort, presently at
 Wieten Staette farm   1/1845

GREVE, --, with w & son-in-law & w; formerly residents at
 "Little" Prues farm   4/1845

BYE, --, s of farmowner -- Bye   1/1845

SCHNEIDHORST, --, s of widow -- Schneidhorst, hired hand;
 dom. Gosekuhlen farms   1/1845

MUEESMANN, --, widow, with family   5/1846

STEINKAMP, Anna Maria, maid   1/1846

BECKER, --, tailor, with w, s, & d (cc under 14 years); not
 property owners   4/1849

DECKER, Molan, with family (2 cc under 15 years); not property owners   5/1849

MESCHER, Bernard, hired hand   1/1849

MESCHER, Heinrich, hired hand   1/1849

MESCHER, Elisabeth, maid   1/1849

Grapperhausen Farming Community

RENNEKER, Bernard, with family; serfs of Gers-Grapperhaus   3/1832

MEYER, Heinrich, with family; serfs at Blomendahl's farm   4/1832

STICKFORT, Friedrich, with family; serfs at Rueter's   4/1834

MESCHER, Gerhard, with family, including son-in-law Josef
    ENGELKE, serfs at Wilken's farm   5/1834

WESSEL, --, farmowner, with family   5/1834

HARDINGHAUS, --, farmowner, with family   2/1835

KREUZMANN, --, 2 dd of Gerd Heinrich Kreuzmann, serfs at
    Bergmann's farm   2/1837

KRAMER, Johann, with 2 ss, serfs at Bergmann's farm   3/1837

THAMANN, Friedrich, with family, serfs at Grapperhaus' farm   8/1837

WESTERHAUS, Berend, with family, serfs at Juergen's farm   4/1838

WESSEL, Heinrich, s of widow -- Wessel, serfs at Johann's
    farm in Wahlde   1/1840

AUF DER HEIDE, Heinrich, with family, including son-in-law
    Heinrich BROCKMANN & his family   8/1844

BROKAMP, Hermann Heinrich, with family, serfs at Juergen's
    farm   3/1844

PIEPER, --, widow, with family, serfs at Gers-Grapperhaus'
    farm   4/1844

BROCKMANN, Berend, with family, serfs from Grapperhaus's
    [farm]   4/1844

WESSEL, --, farmowner, with family; from Kokenwahlde   8/1845

STICKFORT, --, hired hand, with family   4/1845

WESTERHAUS, Berend, with w   2/1845

WEHLAGE, Heinrich   1/1845

Nellinghof Farming Community

MESSMANN, --, farmowner, with w & c, father & mother   5/1834

THAMANN, Dirk, "new" farmowner, with w & 3 cc; lives on the
    land of the prince [*landesherrl. Grund*]   5/1834

WANSTRODT, Heinrich, with w & 6 cc; serfs of Wenstrup's at
    Gers   8/1834

KNABKE, Heinrich, cottage owner, with w & 2 cc   4/1834

WEBER, Hermann, hired hand, with w & 5 cc; dom. Thamann farm 7/1834

SIEFKE, Heinrich, hired hand, with w & 3 cc; dom. Steinkamp
    farm   5/1834

KRONLAGE, Hermann Heinrich, s of Bernd Heinrich Kronlage of
    Schierberg   1/1834

WESSEL, Bernard, s of hired hand Heinrich Wessel at Rehling
    farm   1/1834

DALINGHAUS, Gertrud, Elisabeth, & Bernard Heinrich, cc of the
    "new" farmer Carl Dalinghaus of Nellinghoeferbruch   3/1834

MEYER, Bernard, hired hand, with w & 5 cc; dom. Hellmann's
    cottage   7/1834

REHLING, Gerhard Heinrich, hired hand, with 5 cc; dom.
    Rehling farm   6/1834

WENSTRUP, Carolina & Catharina, dd of farmowner -- Jans-
    Wenstrup   2/1834

DEPEWEG, --, 2 dd of Bernd Depeweg, serfs of Wieghaus' farm 2/1834

LINDEMANN, Catharina, d of hired hand Bernard Lindemann; dom.
    with Johann's in Wenstrup   1/1834

BUSSMANN, Gertrud, d of Bernd Bussmann; dom. Thamann farm   1/1834

MEYER, Elisabeth, d of Bernd Meyer; dom. Johanns' in Wen-
    strup   1/1834

SCHOENHOEFET, Josef, s of Gerd Schoenhoefet; dom. with Gers
    in Wenstrup   1/1834

Nellinghof Farming Community (continued)

MOELLER, Friedrich, s of Bernd Moeller; dom. Erdbrueggen
    farm   1/1834

BUSSMANN, Josef; dom. Steinkamp farm   1/1834

OESTERMANN, Heinrich, tenant, with w & 2 cc; dom. Wanstradt
    farm   4/1835

WANSTRADT, Dirk, s of farmowner Bernd Wanstradt   1/1835

SIEFKE, Gertrud, d of widow -- Siefke; dom. Meyer farm   1/1835

DALINGHAUS, Franz, tenant, with w & 4 cc; dom. Gruending
    farm   6/1835

STEINKAMP, Heinrich, tenant, with w & 4 cc; dom. Gruending
    farm   6/1835

MEYER, Elisabeth & Catharina, dd of tenant Friedrich Meyer;
    dom. Meyer farm   2/1835

MESSMANN, Bernard, tenant at Thamann farm, with son-in-law
    Bernd Heinrich VON DREHLE, with w & 1 c   4/1836

VON DREHLE, Gertrud, d of Bernd von Drehle; dom. Ellerbrock
    farm   1/1836

KROEGER, Heinrich, tenant, with w & 5 cc; dom. Lienesch farm 7/1836

KNABKE, Friedrich, s of cottage owner Heinrich Knabke   1/1836

KNABKE, Bernard, s of cottage owner -- Knabke   1/1837

MEYER, Friedrich, with w, s & the latter's w & 1 c; dom.
    Meyer farm   5/1837

WESSEL, Heinrich, s of tenant Heinrich Wessel; dom. Rehling
    farm   1/1837

KURZHALS, Johann, tenant, with w, son-in-law & [the latter's?]
    3 cc; dom. Erdbruegge farm   6/1837

REHLING, Heinrich & Bernard, ss of Bernard Rehling; dom.
    Wanstradt farm   2/1837

Nellinghof Farming Community (continued)

BROCKMANN, Elisabeth, d of Heinrich Brockmann; dom. Suhren-
brock farm   1/1837

Nellinghof

MUELLER, Josef, with w & 3 cc; from the Heide [Heath]   5/1837

OESTERMANN, Heinrich, s of widow -- Oestermann; Meyer farm   1/1837

VON DREHLE, Bernd, s of Bernd von Drehle [Senior]; dom. Eller-
brock farm   1/1837

KRONLAGE, Josef, s of farmowner -- Kronlage, with w   2/1837

BOCKHORST, Elisabeth, d of Bernd Bockhorst; dom. Steinkamp
farm   1/1837

REHLING, Hermann Heinrich, s of farmowner -- Rehling   1/1838

MEYER, Heinrich, s of Bernd Meyer; dom. with Johann's in
Wenstrup   1/1838

MEYER, Elisabeth, d of Heinrich Meyer; dom. Meyer farm   1/1839

TRIMPE, Friedrich, hired hand, with w; dom. Schuermann farm 2/1839

WESSENDORF, Anton, s of widow -- Wessendorf; dom. Nelling-
hoeferbruch   1/1839

NARBERHAUS, Elisabeth, d of Bernard Narberhaus; dom. Beck-
mann farm   1/1840

SIEFKE, Anna Maria & Catharina, dd of widow -- Siefke; dom.
Meyer farm   2/1841

HUESMANN, Friedrich, with w; dom. with Wieghaus   2/1841

MEYER, Bernard, s of Bernard Meyer [Senior]; dom. Johann's
farm in Wenstrup   1/1841

BROCKMANN, Bernard, s of Bernard Brockmann [Senior]; dom.
Schuermann farm   1/1841

Nellinghof (continued)

FELDMANN, Theodor, serf of Lienesch   1/1841

WENSTRUP, Heinrich, s of Bernd Wenstrup of Schierberg   1/1842

STEINKAMP, Friedrich, hired hand, with w & 1 c; dom. Stein-
    kamp's farm tenant houses   3/1842

BOCKHORST, Elisabeth, d of Bernd Bockhorst; dom. with Stein-
    kamp   1/1842

BROCKMANN, Heinrich, s of Bernd Brockmann; dom. Krolage [so
    spelled] farm   1/1842

HOEDEBECK, Elisabeth, d of farmowner -- Hoedebeck   1/1842

NIENABER, Gertrud, serf of Schuermann   1/1842

VON DREHLE, Josef, serf of Ellerbrock   1/1842

POHLMANN, Friedrich, s of cottage owner -- Pohlmann   1/1842

NARBERHAUS, Heinrich, s of Bernd Narberhaus, serf of Brock-
    mann   1/1842

MESSKER, Gerhard, s of Bernd Messker, serf of Moehlenhoff   1/1843

WESSENDORF, Bernard, s of widow -- Wessendorf from dem
    Bruche   1/1843

SCHNICKE, August, s of miller -- Schnicke   1/1843

KROEGER, Heinrich, with w & 2 cc, serfs of Lienesch   4/1843

BROCKMANN, Maria & Catharina, dd of widow -- Brockmann,
    serfs of Suhrenbrock   2/1843

VON MESSKE, Heinrich, Josef, & Bernard Heinrich, ss of
    Theodor von Messke; dom. Meyer farm   3/1844

BROCKMANN, --, widow, with her s Bernd Brockmann & her
    son-in-law Heinrich KREINEST, with the latter's w
    & 1 c   5/1844

BRANKAMP, Bernd, with w, 3 cc, & mother-in-law Gertrud
    SIEFKE, hired hands at Meyer farm   7/1844

Nellinghof (continued)

WESTERHAUS, Bernd, serf of Thamann	1/1844
THAMANN, Friedrich, s of farmowner -- Thamann	1/1844
KROLAGE, Heinrich, s of farmowner -- Krolage	1/1844
WANSTRADT, Friedrich, s of farmowner -- Wanstradt	1/1844
GRAPPERHAUS, Friedrich, s of Heinrich Grapperhaus, serf of Schoenfeldt	1/1844
REHLING, Friedrich, s of Bernard Rehling; dom. with Wanstradt	1/1844
NURRE, Hermann Heinrich, serf of Ellerbrock	1/1844
KAVEMANN, Carl, s of Heinrich Kavemann; dom. with Helmich	1/1844
SUHRENBROCK, Heinrich, s of Heinrich Suhrenbrock [Senior]; dom. with Helmich	1/1844
WANSTRADT, Catharina, d of Dirk Wanstradt of Schierberge	1/1844
MEYER, Johann, s of Berend Meyer, serf of Johann in Wenstrup	1/1844
MESSMANN, Elisabeth, d of widow -- Messmann; dom. with Wanstradt	1/1844
BOCKHORST, Bernard, with w & 2 dd; dom. Gruending farm	4/1844
FLOTTEMESCH, Johann, s of Josef Flottemesch, hired hand; dom. Meyer farm	1/1844
BERGMANN, Catharina; dom. Bergmann farm	1/1844
WANSTRADT, Josef, with w; dom. with Wanstradt	2/1844
MEYER, Friedrich, Heinrich, & Catharina; dom. Rehling's tenant houses	3/1844
KNABKE, Friedrich, with w & 4 cc	6/1844
SPECKBAUCH, Josef, s of Bernd Speckbauch, serfs of Erdbrueggen	1/1844

Nellinghof (continued)

WESSEL, Josef & Gertrud, s & d of Heinrich Wessel; dom. Rehling farm   2/1844

SCHWINER, Heinrich, s of Heinrich Schwiner [Senior], serf of
Wenstrup   1/1844

WESSEL, Theodor, with w; from Flottemesch   2/1844

KAVEMANN, --, farm owner, with w & 1 s   3/1845

HOEDEBECK, --, d of farm owner -- Hoedebeck   1/1845

NARBERHAUS, --, d of -- Narberhaus from dem Bruche   1/1845

WOBBELER, --, hired hand?; dom. Gers in Wenstrup   1/1845

BROCKMANN, --, d of Bernd Brockmann, serf of Schuermann   1/1845

WOBBELER, --, with family (2 adults & 3 cc); dom. Gers in
Wenstrup (28 March)   5/1846

SEXTRO, Dirk, with family (2 adults &   ; from Gruending's
farms   5/1846

MEYER, --, d of Bernd Meyer from Hoffestadt; dom. Johann's
in Wenstrup (28 March)   1/1846

SEXTRO, Cathrina, maid   1/1849

BIDENHARN, Friedrich, hired hand; also subject to military
service   1/1849

BIDENHARN, Bernd, hired hand   1/1849

KREHE, Bernd, hired hand   1/1849

WANSTRATH, Dirk, hired hand   1/1849

EKELMANN, Gerd, hired hand   1/1849

HILGER, Gerhard, hired hand   1/1849

Neuenkirchen Farming Community

LUEBKE-NARBERHAUS, Friedrich, with w; from Narberhausen	2/1841
LUEBKE-NARBERHAUS, Catharina; from Narberhausen	1/1841
LUEBKE-NARBERHAUS, Josef; from Narberhausen	1/1842
STUERENBERG, Anna Maria; dom. Luebke-Narberhaus in Narberhausen	1/1843
ARNS, Anton; dom. Knapp cottage in Neuenkirchen	1/1840
FINKMANN, Christina; dom. Knapp cottage in Neuenkirchen	1/1840
FINKMANN, Friedrich; dom. Knapp cottage in Neuenkirchen	1/1840
KNAPP, Heinrich, b WINNER, cottage owner, with w & 2 cc & his sister-in-law Catharina Knapp; from Neuenkirchen	5/1836
STEINBECK, Johann Friedrich; dom. Wessel Kramer cottage in Neuenkirchen	1/1830
HUESMANN, Heinrich; dom. Knapp cottage in Neuenkirchen	1/1834
HUESMANN, Heinrich; dom. Knapp cottage in Neuenkirchen [duplicate entry?]	1/1834
STUERENBERG, Heinrich; dom. Luebke-Narberhaus farm, Narberhausen	1/1843
HUESMANN, Heinrich; dom. Knapp cottage in Neuenkirchen	1/1834
HUESMANN, Elisabeth; dom. Knapp cottage in Neuenkirchen	1/1834
MOELLENHOF, Friedrich; dom. Schneidhorst farm in Neuenkirchen	1/1844
NURRE, Catharina, b MOORMANN, married woman; of Neuenkirchen	1/1842
NURRE, Johann Heinrich, of Neuenkirchen	1/1833
NURRE, Bernard Josef & Gertrud, of Neuenkirchen	2/1839
MEYER, Johann Heinrich, hereditary lessee; dom. Moormann farm at Neuenkirchen	1/1830

Neuenkirchen Farming Community (continued)

MEYER, --, w of Johann Heinrich Meyer [*see* previous entry] with
7 cc; dom. Moormann farm at Neuenkirchen   8/1843

BERTING, Anton; dom. Muesmann farm at Neuenkirchen   1/1836

BERTING, Josef; dom. Muesmann farm at Neuenkirchen   1/1843

SCHIERBERG, Heinrich; dom. Muesmann farm at Neuenkirchen   1/1844

BIDENHARN *sive* [formerly?] KRUEMPELMANN, Franz, from Neuenkirchen   1/1836

BIDENHARN, Lisette, sister of the above; from Neuenkirchen   1/1834

VON HEESE, Ludwig, with w & 6 cc; dom. Rolfs bei der Hake
farm at Neuenkirchen   8/1834

NEDDERMEYER, Carl; dom. Rolfs bei der Hake farm at Neuenkirchen   1/1834

ROLFS BEI DER HAKE, Heinrich, farm owner; from Neuenkirchen 1/1834

TANGEMANN, Bernd, hereditary lessee; dom. Rolfs bei der Hake
farm at Neuenkirchen   1/1836

JOHANNESMEYER, Wilhelm, hereditary lessee, with w & mother-
in-law; dom. Rolfs bei der Hake farm at Neuenkirchen   3/1844

KATE, Heinrich, hired hand, with w & 3 cc; dom. with Rudolf
Jakob Meyer at Neuenkirchen   5/1836

LINDEMANN, Hermann Josef; dom. with Rudolf Jakob Meyer at
Neuenkirchen   1/1833

BUNKE, Josef, cottage owner, with w & 4 cc; from Neuenkirchen   6/1840

BUNKE, Gertrud, Anna Maria, & Catharina; from Neuenkirchen   3/1840

OEVERMANN, Elisabeth, d of farm owner -- Oevermann in Neustadt   1/1844

PIEPER, Friedrich, cottage owner, with w & 3 cc; dom. in
Neustadt   5/1844

Neuenkirchen Farming Community (continued)

PIEPER, Franz, from Neustadt	1/1837
PIEPER, Heinrich, from Neustadt	1/1836
PIEPER, Jakob & Bernard, brothers, from Neustadt	2/1844
MOELLER, Anton, hereditary lessee, with w & 2 cc; dom. Oevermann farm at Neustadt	4/1834
TANGEMANN, Heinrich, tenant, with w & 2 cc; dom. Huesmann farm	4/1834
NIEHAUS, Elisabeth; dom. Oevermann farm at Neustadt	1/1834
NIEHAUS, Catharina; dom. Oevermann farm at Neustadt	1/1835
NIEHAUS, Anna Maria; dom Oevermann farm at Neustadt	1/1840
WINNER, Franz, with w & 3 cc; dom. Huesmann farm at Neustadt	5/1834
HUESMANN, --, widow of farm owner -- Huesmann; dom. Huesmann farm at Neustadt	1/1834
GROTE, Heinrich, tenant, with w & 1 c; dom. Winner farm at Neustadt	3/1836
KNABKE, Josef; dom. Winner farm at Neustadt	1/1836
KNABKE, Anton; dom. Winner farm at Neustadt	1/1837
KNABKE, Franz & Bernard, brothers; dom. Winner farm at Neustadt	1/1838
RICHTER, Heinrich, tenant, with w & 1 c; dom. Winner farm at Neustadt	3/1836
WINNER, --, widow, with 4 cc; dom. Winner farm at Neustadt	5/1843
KLEEFOET, Bernard, with w; from Neustadt	2/1831
KLEEFOET, Friedrich; dom. ?	1/1835
SCHIERBERG, --, widow, with 4 cc; dom. Taubke-Westerhaus farm at Westerhausen	5/1834

Neuenkirchen Farming Community (continued)

MOELLER, Friedrich, "new" farm owner, with w & 6 cc	8/1836
BOESCHER, Bernard, from Neuenkirchen	1/1842
HUGENBERG, Friedrich, from Neuenkirchen	1/1839
HUGENBERG, Maria Anna, from Neuenkirchen	1/1843
HUGENBERG, Anton, from Neuenkirchen	1/1844
HUGENBERG, Gertrud, from Neuenkirchen	1/1844
HUESMANN, Gertrud, from Neuenkirchen	1/1844
HUESMANN, Bernard, tenant, with w & 5 cc; dom. Huesmann farm at Neuenkirchen	7/1844
ALBRECHT, Wilhelm; dom. Meyer farm "on church lands" [*in seligen Hofe*] at Neuenkirchen	1/1842
SPANGENBERG, Friedrich; dom. Meyer farm "on church lands" at Neuenkirchen	1/1843
ALBRECHT, Heinrich; dom. Meyer farm "on church lands" at Neuenkirchen	1/1841
MEYER, Friedrich, tenant, with w & 3 cc; dom. Meyer farm "on church lands" at Neuenkirchen	5/1843
LANGENKAMP, Bernard, from Narberhausen	1/1843
LANGENKAMP, Gertrud, from Narberhausen	1/1843
LANGENKAMP, Catharina, from Narberhausen	1/1844
KOENIG, Gertrud, from Narberhausen	1/1843
WIEGHAUS, Catharina, from Narberhausen	1/1843
PETERSEN, Ludwig, from Narberhausen	1/1842
BACK, Josef, property owner, of Neuenkirchen	1/1832
BACK, --, wife, from Neuenkirchen	1/1844

Neuenkirchen Farming Community (continued)

CLAUSTERMANN, Catharina, from Neuenkirchen	1/1842
STEINKAMP, Josef, with w & 3 cc, from Neuenkirchen	5/1844
HEUSMANN, Bernd, "new" farmer, with w & 6 cc, from Neuenkirchen	8/1844
FLOTTEMESCH, Bernd, from Neuenkirchen	1/1843
HUESMANN, Heinrich; dom. Luenne cottage in Neuenkirchen	1/1842
WELAGE, Josef, from Neuenkirchen	1/1830
HUSSMANN, Heinrich; dom. with Gerd Welage at Neuenkirchen	1/1830
RECHTIEN, Ludwig, from Neuenkirchen	1/1844
WEDEKIND, Christian, from Neuenkirchen	1/1844
SCHIERBERG, Gertrud, from Neustadt	1/1834
HELWIG, Friedrich; dom. with Schierberg in Neuenkirchen	1/1842
NURRENBROCK, Josef, from Neuenkirchen	1/1844
BRUEGGEMANN, Josef, from Neuenkirchen	1/1841
KREKE, Friedrich, hereditary lessee, with w & 2 cc, from Neuenkirchen	4/1842
SEELING, --, widow, & 4 cc EIGNER; from Neustadt	5/1834
SETLAGE, --, widow, & 5 cc; dom. with Bidenharn in Neuenkirchen	6/1842
KAETER, Bernd, with w, from Neuenkirchen	2/1835
IGELMANN, Friedrich; dom. with Knollenberg in Neuenkirchen	1/1840
WIGGER, Heinrich, from Neuenkirchen	1/1832
OEVERMANN, Heinrich; dom. Taube farm at Westerhausen	1/1834
OEVERMANN, Bernd; dom. Taube farm at Westerhausen	1/1836

Neuenkirchen Farming Community (continued)

OEVERMANN, Friedrich; dom. Taube farm at Westerhausen   1/1841

OEVERMANN, Elisabeth; dom. Taube farm at Westerhausen   1/1834

OEVERMANN, Catharina; dom. Taube farm at Westerhausen   1/1840

OEVERMANN, Gertrud; dom. Taube farm at Westerhausen   1/1839

GREVE, Franz; dom. Taube farm at Westerhausen   1/1843

GREFER, Catharina; dom Taube farm at Westerhausen   1/1838

HUELSMANN, Josef; dom. Taube farm at Westerhausen   1/1843

VELTMANN, Bernd; dom. Taube farm at Westerhausen   1/1843

VELTMANN, Anna Margaretha; dom. Taube farm at Westerhausen   1/1843

GREFENKAMP, Agnes; dom. Taube farm at Westerhausen   1/1838

DIEKHAUS, Friedrich, from Neuenkirchen   1/1842

FINKMANN, Ludwig, tenant, with w & 4 cc; dom. with Rudolf
    Jakob Meyer in Neuenkirchen   6/1837

RENNEKER, Anna Maria, from Neuenkirchen   1/1842

BUSSMANN, Elisabeth; dom. with Friedrich Bidenharn in Neuen-
    kirchen   1/1843

WESTENDORF, Anton; dom. with shoe repairman -- Kampke in
    Neuenkirchen   1/1842

SCHMIDTWILKE, Friedrich, cottage owner, in Neuenkirchen   1/1836

WINNER, Josef; dom. with Friedrich Bidenharn in Neuenkirchen   1/1838

HANENKAMP, Gerd, "new" farm owner, with w   2/1836

BERGNER, Chourse [so spelled], from Neuenkirchen   1/1836

TIMMERMANN, Gerhard; dom. Welage farm at Neuenkirchen   1/1834

VON WAHLDE, Margaretha Maria, from Neuenkirchen   1/1834

Neuenkirchen Farming Community (continued)

LUKS, Bernard; formerly with Lokenberg in Neuenkirchen	1/1834
BIDENHARN, Johann Friedrich, in Neuenkirchen	1/1831
BIDENHARN, Bernardina, from Neuenkirchen	1/1833
STUERENBERG, --, widow	1/1845
MORGENROTH, --, tailor	1/1845
HULSMANN, Catharina	1/1845
LANGENKAMP, --, former farm owner, [with family?]	5/1846
LUEBKE-NARBERHAUS, Berend	1/1846
FELDMANN, Elisabeth	1/1846
BIDENHARN, Bernard	1/1846
IGELMANN, --, widow, with s & d (both over 15 years); not property owners; took 100 Reichsthaler with them; they emigrated to join sons who had left years ago	3/1846
SEHLE, --, widow, day laborer, unattached, not a property owner	1/1846
SCHIERBERG, Catharina, maid	1/1846
HUGENBERG, Carolina	1/1846
SPECKING, Elisabeth, maid	1/1846
BRABAND, August, goldsmith	1/1846
KREYENHAGEN, Eduard, shop clerk	1/1846
SCHMIDT, Gerd, day laborer, with [w?] & 1 s & 1 d (both under 15 years)	4/1847
MORGENROTH, Julie, maid	1/1847
FLOTTEMESCH, Josef, hired hand	1/1847
NARBERHAUS, Berend Heinrich, hired hand	1/1847

Neuenkirchen Farming Community (continued)

WIECHHAUS, Catharina, maid   1/1847

BROCKMANN, Berend, day laborer, with [w?] & 6 cc (3 cc under
    15 years)   8/1847

RECHTIEN, Heinrich, tailor, with [w?] & 1 d (under 15 years);
    they emigrated to America on the advice of their sons
    who had emigrated before them & who sent them the passage
    money   3/1847

MIDDENDORF, Josef, hired hand; took 275 Reichsthaler with him1/1847

SPECKBAUCH, Friedrich, & his sister; hired hands   2/1847

LINDEMANN, Friedrich, hired hand   1/1847

SCHWENER, Maria, maid   1/1847

NOBBE, Christian, blacksmith, with [w?], 2 ss, & 1 d; not a
    property owner   5/1848

KLOSTERMANN, hired hand, seeking a better future   1/1848

WINNER, Josef, hired hand, seeking a better future   1/1848

WANSTRAT, Josef, hired hand, seeking a better future   1/1848

KROLAGE, Bernd, hired hand, seeking a better future   1/1848

BIDENHARN, Lisabeth, maid, seeking a better future   1/1848

MUSTERMANN, Adelheid, maid, seeking a better future   1/1848

WESSEL, Anton, of Flottemesch, emigrated in the fall of 1848
    to America but died at Bremerhafen   1/1848

MAAG, Friedrich, with [w?], 4 ss, & 4 dd (2 cc under 15 years);
    not property owners   10/1849

KREUZMANN, Josef, hand laborer, with w, s, & d (under 15
    years); not property owners   4/1849

OEVERMANN, Dina, maid   1/1849

Neuenkirchen Farming Community (continued)

BROCKMANN, Anna Maria, maid   1/1849

FELDMANN, Catharina, sewing woman   1/1849

MORGENROTH, Friedrich, emigrated to avoid military service   1/1849

MESTEMAKER, Josef, emigrated to avoid military service   1/1849

LAGEMANN, Josef, hired hand, emigrated to avoid military service   1/1849

BECKMANN, Bernd, hired hand, emigrated to avoid military ser-
vic   1/1849

BROCKMANN, Berend, with [w?], 2 ss, & 2 dd (under 15 years);
peasants, not property owners   6/1849

Surname Index